Dancing with Saddam

D1566231

Dancing with Saddam

The Strategic Tango of Jordanian–Iraqi Relations

David Schenker

THE WASHINGTON INSTITUTE
FOR NEAR EAST POLICY
Washington, D.C.

LEXINGTON BOOKS
Lanham • Boulder • New York • Oxford

LEXINGTON BOOKS

Published in the United States of America
by Lexington Books
An imprint of The Rowman & Littlefield Publishing Group, Inc.
4501 Forbes Boulevard, Suite 200, Lanham, Maryland 20706

PO Box 317, Oxford, OX2 9RU, UK

Published in cooperation with The Washington Institute for Near East Policy
1828 L Street NW, Suite 1050
Washington, D.C. 20036

British Library Cataloguing in Publication Information Available

Library of Congress Cataloging-in-Publication Data

Schenker, David Kenneth, 1968–
  Dancing with Saddam : the strategic tango of Jordanian-Iraqi relations /
David Schenker.
       p. cm.
  Includes bibliographical references and index.
  ISBN 0-7391-0648-1 — ISBN 0-7391-0649-X (pbk.)
  1. Jordan—Relations—Iraq. 2. Iraq—Relations—Jordan. I. Title.
  DS154.16.I72S34   2003
  327.56950567—dc21   2003005605

Printed in the United States of America

∞™ The paper used in this publication meets the minimum requirements of American
National Standard for Information Sciences—Permanence of Paper for Printed Library
Materials, ANSI/NISO Z39.48-1992.

Contents

Acknowledgments

This study is the product of research conducted during 1999–2001 while I was a fellow at the Washington Institute for Near East Policy. The project was conceived in 1998 during discussions with friends and colleagues—in particular with Professor Abbas Kelidar—and was completed prior to my departure from the Institute in December 2001.

The list of those to whom I am indebted is long and starts at the Washington Institute. During my tenure at the institute, Executive Director Robert Satloff was an ideal boss and an excellent editor. Rob's suggestions and sharp editor's pen improved the body of my writings in the years 1998–2001. This study is no exception. The book also benefited from the careful readings and suggestions of Institute deputy director Patrick Clawson.

In addition to my colleagues at the institute, I would also like to thank Marin Strmecki and the Smith Richardson Foundation for their generous support of this project.

In no small part, this study benefited from the insight gained during two trips to Jordan. In this regard, I am deeply indebted to the dozens of Jordanian politicians, businessmen, intellectuals, and royals who spoke with me about a subject that, along with the topic of Jordanian Palestinians, ranks among the more sensitive issues in the Kingdom. Respect for confidentiality precludes the mention of names, but this does not diminish my gratitude.

In particular, however, I would like to thank the unabashedly pro-Saddam Khaldoun Abu Hassan, then chairman of the Amman Chamber of Industry. Despite our diametrically opposed views, Mr. Abu Hassan generously volunteered his time and the resources of his organization to assist with this project. The chamber's statistics and its chairman's views were an invaluable addition to this study.

In addition to these interviewees, I bear a debt of gratitude to Washington Institute Soref Fellow Avi Jorisch, for assisting with (i.e., correcting) my transliterations, and to Ashraf Zeitoon, an aspiring young Jordanian scholar who provided helpful research assistance. Likewise, Institute publications staff Alicia Gansz and George Lopez were, as always, a pleasure to work with.

When my first book was published in 2000, I took the opportunity to thank a cadre of friends and mentors. This group—and a few unnamed but significant others—remains an important influence in my life and on my thinking, and I am grateful. I would also like to express gratitude to my family for their consistent love and encouragement.

Last, but certainly not least, I would like to acknowledge my fiancée and future wife, Jodi Danis. Jodi has for years been my leading supporter and chief counsel. Her patience and perseverance is extraordinary, and I am truly lucky to have found her.

Today as I write these acknowledgments, I serve as an adviser in the Office of the Secretary of Defense at the Pentagon, where among other things, part of my area of responsibility is Jordan. As is customary and obligatory, I should say that this book, which will be published more than a year after my entrance into government, is not a reflection or statement of U.S. government policy. The views expressed herein are mine alone.

With the exception of a few minor updates based on public domain material made in October 2002, the book—including the section on policy recommendations—was written prior to my government service.

While the interviews and insight from my colleagues were invaluable, I alone bear responsibility for the content and deficiencies of the text. Translations from the Arabic are mine unless otherwise indicated.

Transliteration note: This study employs a system based on that of the *International Journal of Middle East Studies* (IJMES). The only diacritical marks used are *'ayn*, indicated by ', and *hamza*, indicated by ', and only when they appear in the middle of a word.

Introduction

Of all the states bordering Iraq, none has a set of bilateral relations with Baghdad as complex as does the Hashemite Kingdom of Jordan. These ties exist on several levels. Historically, while the regions that eventually became the modern-day countries of Iraq and Jordan were governed as separate parts of the Ottoman Empire, they came together under the rule of different branches of the Hashemite family from 1921 through 1958. Culturally, Baghdad's traditional orientation has been toward the Fertile Crescent,[1] not toward the Persian Gulf, as is commonly assumed. And economically, Amman and Baghdad have grown ever closer together, evidenced by Jordan's role as Iraq's principal entrepôt, a position it has held for more than twenty years.

But, despite the appearance of synergy, the relationship has not been one of equals. Although it has been at war or severely limited or both by international sanctions since 1990, Iraq is a wealthy state with large reserves of oil, two mighty rivers, and a population of 24 million. Jordan, on the other hand, is a poor state, with less than a quarter of Iraq's population and without much in the way of water or other natural resources. These asymmetries have fostered a predictable dynamic. Over the years, Jordan has become economically dependent on Iraq. In turn, Iraqi influence in Jordan has grown strong.

The radical nature of Iraqi politics under President Saddam Hussein has placed Jordan in a precarious position. Since its establishment, Jordan's existence has been predicated on the Hashemites' ability to balance between the regional forces of extremism and moderation. Jordan has contended with a Palestinian population widely believed to constitute 60 percent of the Kingdom. At the same time, the country has maintained good ties with Iraq, the United States, and Israel.

Jordan's relative disadvantage was exacerbated in February 1999 by the death of King Hussein, who had reigned for nearly five decades. Against all

1

odds, King Hussein had kept the Kingdom afloat among a sea of adversaries, including Palestine Liberation Organization chairman (and later Palestinian Authority *ra'is*) Yasser Arafat and Syrian president Hafez al-Assad. Since 1979, King Hussein also had to contend with Jordan's sometime friend and sometime foe in Baghdad—Saddam Hussein. On his death, King Hussein was succeeded by his eldest son Abdullah, who, until that point, had served in the military and had little experience in political matters.

While succession went smoothly, uncertainty prevailed in the realm. How would Abdullah fare against the likes of Saddam?

Almost immediately after his ascent to the throne, King Abdullah set out to address some of the more pressing economic problems facing Jordan. Saddled with debt, plagued with high unemployment, and faced with a sadly stagnant economy, boosting development became the number one priority on Abdullah's agenda. In addition to implementing some deep economic reforms, the new king pursued two initiatives designed to improve the economy. First, he sought to strengthen Jordan's economic relations with the United States. Part of this plan entailed seeking additional foreign assistance dollars. At the same time, the king turned to Iraq—which until that time had been Jordan's largest source of aid—for additional assistance. To this end, in the initial years of his reign, King Abdullah sought to enhance the Kingdom's trade ties with Baghdad.

It is easy to understand the Jordanian attraction to Iraq. But economic dependence on Baghdad—and by extension on the largesse of Saddam—has not been without its perils to the Jordanian regime. For example, in 2001, Iraq—Jordan's sole supplier of oil—raised its prices from $19 to $21 per barrel. This minor increase amounted to a $170 million overall increase in the Kingdom's deficit, essentially making Jordan noncompliant with its International Monetary Fund (IMF) reform program commitments. To generate additional revenue and meet its IMF obligations, the Kingdom decided to increase the price of gasoline to Jordanian consumers by 20 percent. However, fear of domestic riots, protests, and other acts of instability forced the regime to opt instead for a 13 percent sales tax that projections indicated would generate enough revenue to cover the oil-price deficit.

That Jordan would be compelled to risk its domestic stability because of Saddam's whim for profit is troubling. Worse, however, is the reality that Saddam has had the economic power to manipulate such situations in Jordan practically at will. In addition to wreaking economic havoc, as the events surrounding the Palestinian uprising against Israel suggest, Saddam also possesses the leverage to foment political instability in the Kingdom.

For Jordan, this dynamic gives reason for anxiety. Yet the implications are also of considerable concern to the United States. Jordan is a pivot between moderate pro-Western states (like Israel and, to a lesser extent, Saudi Arabia) and radical anti-American states (like Iraq and Syria). As such, Jordan has long played the role of the weak but independent buffer state, keeping strong states—like Iraq and Israel—apart. Likewise, over time the Kingdom's Hashemite leaders have, in their own understated fashion, encouraged regional political moderation.

Jordan has been able to play a stabilizing role in the region, in no small part because its leadership has avoided close alignments with its neighbors. But the passing of King Hussein in 1999, the deterioration of the domestic economic situation, and the volatile regional scene have taken their toll on the Kingdom. These factors—coupled with growing Iraqi influence in Jordan, the continuing resonance of Saddam (particularly among Palestinians), and the multiplier effect of new regional satellite news channels that bring the drama of the Palestinian and Iraqi causes to the screens of countless Jordanians (and others throughout the region)—cumulatively threaten to undermine the core of Jordan's independence and skew the neutrality that the Kingdom has endeavored to cultivate. In short, a series of environmental factors have contributed to what has become a very dangerous period in Jordan's history. Among these factors, Iraq has pride of place.

This study attempts to describe and interpret, from the Jordanian perspective, the deep historical, social, political, and economic relationship between Iraq and Jordan. Insofar as this research spans the transition of leadership in Jordan, it also analyzes continuity and change with regard to the Kingdom's Iraq policy from Hussein to Abdullah. More than anything else, this study explores the costs, benefits, and opportunities that the association between the two countries presents for Jordan and for U.S. policy goals in the Middle East.

To be sure, the nature of the Jordanian–Iraqi relationship is complex. To provide a sense of scope with regard to these bilateral ties, this book delves into a broad range of issues. Chapter 1 offers a brief overview of the history and political trends in the Jordanian–Iraqi relationship. Chapter 2 focuses on the most salient aspect of the interaction—economics. Chapter 3 turns to the topic of Iraqi influence, specifically the presence of pro-Iraqi elements in the Kingdom; the ability of these elements to affect policy or to manipulate domestic affairs or both in Jordan is often underestimated. Finally, chapter 4 discusses King Abdullah's Iraq policy since his coronation in February 1999. Taken together, these chapters paint a comprehensive picture of those elements comprising Jordanian–Iraqi relations.

NOTE

1. See, for example, Albert Hourani, *History of the Arab Peoples* (Cambridge, Mass.: Harvard University Press, 1991). See also Charles Issawi, *The Fertile Crescent 1800–1914: A Documentary Economic History* (New York: Oxford University Press, 1988).

Chapter One

History and Common Identity

Jordanian–Iraqi relations today are the product of shared history, common identity, and economic exigency. To be sure, economic factors (the subject of chapter 2) are the primary force driving the close state-to-state relationship that has emerged since the 1980s. Underpinning these ties, however, is a historical context that bonds Jordanians to their Iraqi neighbors.

Despite urbanization, progress toward mass literacy, and modern communications, Jordanian society remains largely tribal in nature. A snapshot of news in the Kingdom—from reports of "honor killings"[1] to demands by Islamist political parties for a change in the electoral law to "de-tribalize" voting patterns—only confirms the ongoing resonance of tribalism in Jordanian society. To dismiss these factors as passé or unimportant would be to negate the social and cultural environment in which Jordan has developed as a modern state and in which Jordanian–Iraqi relations have developed over the past generation.

CROSS-BORDER IDENTITIES

Politically, Iraq and Jordan became intertwined in 1920 when the British Mandatory powers anointed as king of Iraq the scion of the Hashemite sharifian family of Mecca, Faisal. While Hashemite rule ended in Iraq in 1958—with the execution of Faisal II, grandson of Faisal I—the ties between the states and the peoples were not severed. Indeed relationships that existed for centuries (under the Ottomans and the Abbasids before them) seem to have persevered. Even today, Jordanians note that the Kingdom is "an extension of Iraq in geographic terms."[2]

But the bond is deeper than just politics and economics. Jordan and Iraq not only share a common border, they share a common history. As King Hussein

5

himself said in August 1995: "Iraq, its people and soldiers have a special status in the hearts of Jordanians. This status is characterized by sincere brotherhood with which we lived throughout the long march, and which was nourished by the pages of shining history."[3]

While these sentiments have not always translated into Jordanian policy vis-à-vis Iraq, history suggests that popular opinion has been a very strong influence on decision making in the Kingdom, particularly regarding Iraq and Palestinian issues. This calculation contributed to King Hussein's decision to enter the June 1967 War, despite Israel's urging to stay out, and it also influenced Hussein's decision not to ally with the U.S.-led coalition against Saddam in 1991. More recently, these types of pressures have (in tandem with economic exigencies) encouraged King Abdullah to take a leading role in the effort to end international sanctions on Iraq while denying any direct Jordanian role in U.S. efforts to unseat Saddam Hussein.

It is no secret that Jordanians have very strong feelings of amity and friendship toward Iraqis. What is notable, however, is the depth to which these feelings prevail in the Kingdom. Interestingly, Iraq is one of the few subjects on which most all Jordanians—East Bankers and Palestinians alike—agree. Jordanians—even those who loath Saddam—typically articulate a "closeness" between the peoples. As one Jordanian described it, "The mentality of the Iraqi is the same as the Jordanian."[4]

Many in the Kingdom likewise suggest that the past ten years have deepened the historical ties. For example, in 1998, then crown prince Hassan bin Talal said that the relationship between the two countries has "become more special recently due to the deep sense of concern that the Arabs feel with regard to the plight of the Iraqis."[5] Khaldoun Abu Hassan, former chairman of the Amman Chamber of Industry (ACI) and a leading advocate on behalf of Iraq, agrees. He maintains that the "suffering [brought on by the Gulf War and the sanctions] has brought Jordan and Iraq closer."[6]

For Jordanians, the bilateral relationship is about more than just sympathy. "The relations," said Prince Hassan, "can be described as intertwined in the spiritual and national sense."[7] He explained: "We feel a kinship due to the fact that we are geographically and demographically close . . . we are told that we express too much compassion toward the ordinary Iraqi citizen. But how could the case be otherwise?" Hassan's suggestion that the connection was "spiritual" speaks volumes about how the Hashemites perceive relations with Iraq. The ties to Iraq are part of what defines most Jordanians' sense of nation and self; they emerge from personal, emotional, and national duty.

On the sentimental level, as King Hussein has said, Jordanians are "a people who love Iraq and the Iraqi people, and who feel their suffering and live their pain."[8] More than this, however, the king pointed to his family's duties and responsibilities toward Iraq, frequently recalling the origins of the two states and the period when branches of the Hashemite family ruled from Jerusalem to Baghdad. According to King Hussein: "[Iraq's] beginnings and our beginnings here in Jordan were the same beginnings on all levels. It stemmed from the Great Arab Revolt, along with its army and position. It has always been with us, and we have always been with it."[9] These feelings are not solely the province of Jordanian royalty. They resonate with important elements of the Jordanian people.

FROM THE GREAT ARAB REVOLT TO THE IRAN–IRAQ WAR

For average Jordanians, the events of the twentieth century—primarily the Great Arab Revolt and the Arab–Israeli conflict—provide the foundation of the modern bilateral relationship with Iraq. The peoples of what would later become Jordan and Iraq were comrades in arms, both against the Ottoman Empire and, in the later part of the century, against Israel. Based on these shared experiences, many in Amman consider Iraq to be Jordan's "strategic depth"—a sentiment expressed on both the official and the popular level.

In a sense, the 1994 signing of the Israeli–Jordanian peace treaty signaled the end of nearly seventy-five years of Iraqi–Jordanian military cooperation. Prior to 1994, Iraq had, according to former Jordanian prime minister Abdel Salam Majali, always helped the Kingdom to "withstand Israel." Iraq participated alongside Jordan in all the Arab–Israeli wars, for example. In 1949, the Iraqi Expeditionary Force fought in Jerusalem with the Jordanian Arab Legion. This service and cooperation, according to Majali, "is not forgotten."[10]

During each of the three major Arab–Israeli wars—those in 1948, 1967, and 1973—Iraq contributed approximately one-third of its total ground forces to the Arab efforts. In both 1948 and 1967, these troops mobilized toward the Israeli border via Jordanian territory. In 1948 Iraq constituted the largest fighting force in Palestine.[11] Israeli sources maintain that Israel's preemptive attack on Egypt and Syria in 1967 was precipitated by Iraqi troop mobilizations to the Jordan River. And in 1973, Iraqi and Jordanian forces at times fought together in combined units.

More than the wars against Israel, however, the 1916–1920 Great Arab Revolt against the Ottoman Empire created the mythology of Jordanian–Iraqi relations. A collaborative effort, the Arab revolt was essentially a joint Arab–British campaign to end Ottoman rule in the Near East following the Ottoman alliance with Germany in World War I. The Arabs were led by Sharif Hussein, the head of the Hashemite clan whose sons would become founding monarchs of Iraq and Jordan. While the Hashemites led the forces, the officer corps was composed largely of men hailing from territories in current-day Iraq.[12]

Although the Israeli–Jordanian peace treaty—and its prohibition on the entry of third-country military forces without common assent—effectively ended Jordanian–Iraqi military cooperation, the memories and loyalties persevere, primarily via a body of symbols and rituals. There is, for example, a graveyard of Iraqi soldiers in Mafraq in northeastern Jordan. The soldiers buried there were killed in 1948 and 1973 while fighting alongside Jordanian troops against Israel. Since 1948, the mayor of Mafraq, as well as an Iraqi representative in Jordan, visits the graveyard to lay wreaths. Even today this annual event is given recognition on Jordanian evening television news programs.

Iraqi "sacrifices" on the Arab–Israeli front continue to resonate for both Jordanians and Iraqis. For the Hashemites, Iraqi participation is accorded a position of respect and honor. Saddam, too, continues to derive at least rhetorical benefit from Iraq's participation in the wars with Israel. For example, in his March 27, 2001, letter to the Arab Summit in Amman, Saddam alluded to the dead and to their relationship to Jordan. "The graves of Iraqi martyrs are still visited," he said "by Jordanians."[13]

It is difficult to define the importance that most Jordanians accord the Great Arab Revolt in the development of their national identity. Likewise, it is difficult to quantify the affinity and loyalty that characterizes relations between Jordanians and Iraqis today. There are indications, however, that the bonds run deep. For example, the fact that thousands of Jordanians volunteered to serve in the Quwat al-Yarmouk (Yarmouk Forces) on the side of Iraq during the war with Iran points to the ongoing strength of bilateral ties on a popular level. Between 1979 and 1988, up to five thousand Jordanian civilians— retired soldiers, mechanics, and men from all walks of life—volunteered to fight against Iran.

These troops were trained at Jordanian army recruitment centers and paid by the Iraqi government. Throughout the war, many served in noncombatant positions, such as guarding logistics centers in Iraq. As one observer suggested, these forces were essentially a *jaish sha'abi*, a popular army, and joining this army was almost synonymous with fighting for one's own country. Notwithstanding the fact that the Quwat al-Yarmouk were irregular forces that did not meet even the mediocre standards of Iraqi regular army troops, the volunteerism of these several thousand Jordanians was clearly indicative of support for Iraq among the Kingdom's populace.

After the Iran–Iraq War, a measure of official military cooperation between Jordan and Iraq—primarily involving the 1989 training of Jordanian pilots in Iraq on F-1 Mirage aircraft—did occur. According to Israeli sources, this training involved a joint Jordanian–Iraqi air force wing, with Iraqi pilots flying Iraqi airplanes painted with Jordanian colors. These planes flew over the Jordan Valley taking aerial reconnaissance photographs of Israel. At about the same time, Jordanian generals were said to have brought top Iraqi officials to the Jordan Valley to tour the Israeli border area. The Israelis complained bitterly about this cooperation, both to King Hussein and to the United States, and Jordan eventually moved the "training maneuvers" to the Eastern Desert. Interestingly, this instance was perhaps the only time since 1967 that Iraq and Jordan cooperated in a serious military manner against Israel. To this day, it is not entirely clear why this particular cooperation occurred. Some scholars suggest that it may have been related to the resurgence of a "Jordan is Palestine" theme in Israel's national political debate at the time.

On some level it appears that the common historical, military, cultural, and social bonds that connect Jordan and Iraq have had a strategic component too. This aspect of the relationship is most often manifested in the oft-cited Jordanian concept that Iraq constitutes "an important strategic depth for Jordan."[14]

Articulated by King Hussein and after his death by Prince Hassan, this notion appears to be a constant policy talking point for the Hashemite leadership.[15] For the Hashemites, "strategic depth" has had varying connotations. From the 1920s through 1970, Iraq provided the Kingdom with what they described as "depth" against their common Israeli adversary. During the Iran–Iraq War, Jordan provided Iraq with "strategic depth" in the Sunni battle against what was viewed as Shi'ite expansionism. More recently, Jordanian royals confide, Iraq provides Jordan with a "strategic Sunni depth" against the Palestinians.

REAL ARAB NATIONALISM?

With a population widely believed to be at least 60 percent Palestinian, it is not surprising that Saddam Hussein is quite popular in Jordan. As in much of the Arab world, Saddam's appeal to the Jordanian street is largely related to his "Arab nationalist" credentials. In a sense, his continued calls for Arab unity, opposition to any compromise with Israel, and rejection of American regional "hegemony" are reminiscent of the "glory days" of Nasserism.

In the West, Saddam's rhetoric is largely viewed as a cynical ploy to garner support in the Arab world. Regardless of whether this assessment is correct, clearly many Jordanians are convinced that Iraqis are sincere about pan-Arabism. As one former Jordanian official sympathetic to pan-Arabism explained, the Iraqis "are the only believers in this among the Arabs. This is why Iraq continues to help Jordan."[16]

Objectively speaking, Iraq provides Jordan with a lot of "help." This includes discounted oil, pledges to purchase Jordanian products (sometimes at a higher cost than elsewhere, as is the case with palm oil), and commitments to ship products to Iraq via Jordan's lone port, Aqaba, despite the availability of less expensive and more convenient ports in the Persian Gulf. To the average Jordanian—not taking into account the political quid pro quos—it appears that there is no convincing economic rationale for all the "help."

There is, of course, a long history of Iraqi assistance to the Kingdom, much of which Jordanians understand as Iraqi support for pan-Arabism. The pledges made during the March 1979 Baghdad conference provide a good example. At that meeting, held to provide support to those states that refused to participate in U.S.-brokered Arab–Israeli peacemaking of the sort that led to the Egyptian–Israeli peace treaty, an Arab "support fund" was established to disburse funds to Syria, Jordan, and the Palestine Liberation Organization—the "front line" in the confrontation with Israel. The annual allocation for Jordan was set at $1.2 billion. Of the contributing states—which included Saudi Arabia and a few Persian Gulf sheikhdoms, as well as Libya, Algeria, and Iraq—only Iraq and Oman had fulfilled their pledges by the end of 1979, and only Jordan seemed to have received its promised sums.[17]

Saddam Hussein, too, has recognized the significance to Jordanians of Hashemite history in Iraq. In July 1980 during a visit to Baghdad, King Hussein and Saddam visited the Hashemite graveyard where Faisal I was buried. Later, Saddam allocated over $3 million for the renovation of the cemetery. While this appeared to be a blatantly cynical ploy to cement burgeoning relations with Amman, it nevertheless highlights the importance of such symbols in the relationship.

Interestingly, although many of Saddam's supporters in the Kingdom recognize that Saddam himself is responsible for the suffering of the Iraqi people, this realization appears to have had little demonstrable effect on his overall popularity among Jordanians. The Jordanian political elite—that is, East Bankers who recognize the importance of maintaining strategic ties to the West (and to Israel)—are somewhat embarrassed by the continued high regard for Saddam in the Kingdom. One Jordanian diplomat in Washington explained, "Jordanians love the symbol—they do not love Saddam." Jordanians do appear to be more pro-Iraqi than pro-Saddam. But as one Jordanian business magnate observed, "they can hardly support the US vs. Saddam."[18]

In Jordan it is difficult to distinguish the true popular resonance of Saddam the symbol versus Saddam the ruthless dictator. As Aida Dabbas, spokesperson for the National Mobilization Committee for the Defense of Iraq, describes it, Saddam is more popular than ever in the Kingdom. In April 2000, Dabbas directed what was called the Pencil Campaign, traveling from Um Qais to Aqaba collecting millions of pencils for Iraqi children allegedly languishing without even the most basic educational materials. According to Dabbas, latent support for Saddam—and a healthy resentment if not hatred toward the United States—is the norm among Jordanians. This is especially the case in southern Jordan, she said, where most people would "die for Saddam."[19]

These sentiments contrast sharply with what Jordanians typically express about their northern neighbors, the Syrians. Certainly, official relations between Syria under the late President Hafez al-Assad and Jordan under the late King Hussein were, at best, cold. Prior to the April 2000 Jordanian–Syrian "rapprochement" under the new leadership (King Abdullah in Jordan and Bashar al-Assad in Syria), there had been a long history of Syrian attempts to destabilize King Hussein's regime and a regular onslaught of official insults emanating from Damascus toward Amman. In October 1998, for example, Syrian defense minister Mustafa Tlass opined that there was no such country as Jordan. Jordan, he said, was merely "south Syria."

In terms of rhetoric and optics, Jordanian–Syrian relations improved after King Abdullah and Bashar al-Assad took over. Indeed, shortly after the new leaders assumed power, press stories appeared describing how the king and the new Syrian dictator were tooling around Amman in one of the king's sports cars. Despite promising beginnings, however, problems with Syrian infiltrations into Jordan persisted through the leadership transition in both countries, and a renaissance in bilateral state-to-state relations never materialized.

On the popular level, perhaps the best indications of how Jordanians perceive Syrians are the events surrounding the "Ocalan affair." After years of protesting Damascus's support for Kurdish terrorism, Turkey massed troops on Syria's northern border in September 1998 and threatened to invade if Kurdistan Workers' Party (PKK) leader Abdullah Ocalan were not expelled from the Syrian capital. Despite the threat of an attack on a "sister" Arab state by the inheritors of the "hated Ottomans," Jordanians yawned; there was little if any notable public reaction. In fact, aside from a few pro-Syrian commentaries written by the usual (pro-Iraqi) suspects, there was no public outcry in Jordan about the Turkish threat.

HISTORICAL PERSPECTIVE: PROLOGUE TO THE GULF WAR

Since Jordan and Iraq were established as autonomous political entities in the early part of the twentieth century, relations between the two countries have vacillated between the extremes of close friendship and overt hostility. Historically, two factors have shaped the relationship: economic imperatives and Jordan's dealings with its other neighbors, particularly the Syrians and Palestinians.

From 1932 to 1958, when Jordan and Iraq were both ruled by Hashemite monarchs, relations were cordial, even if sometimes strained by the imbalance of power between the two branches of the family and the far greater importance that the dominant British gave to Iraq than to Jordan. Bilateral relations soured in 1958 when Iraqi Ba'thists killed twenty-five members of the Hashemite family—including the king—in a coup d'etat that deposed the monarchy. The relationship declined even further with the rise of Abdel Salaam Aref in Baghdad, whose undeclared aim, many in Jordan believed, was the removal of the Hashemites in Amman.

In subsequent years, propelled by economic and geopolitical imperatives— particularly the emergence of Nasserism as a regional phenomenon in the 1960s and the rift between the Iraqi and Syrian Ba'thists—Jordan's King Hussein pursued and achieved a pragmatic modus vivendi with Iraq. The appointment of Wasfi al-Tel, a Jordanian of Kurdish descent, as ambassador to Iraq smoothed relations in the early 1960s, and by the mid-1970s, Iraq was providing Jordan with development assistance. After Saddam's rise to power and particularly during the Iran–Iraq War (1980–1988), relations flourished into a full rapprochement. Dependent on Jordan for war materiel and port facilities, Iraq became Jordan's top trade partner and number one source of financial aid throughout the 1980s. Indeed, by 1985—the heyday of trade relations—Iraq accounted for nearly half of Jordan's nonmineral exports, or $168.7 million.[20] During these years, Jordan's economic infrastructure was redesigned to primarily support Iraq's financial and economic needs while the Jordanian labor force shifted to provide Iraq's industrial and service needs.[21]

Likewise, prior to the 1991 Gulf War, Jordan was receiving nearly 85 percent of its oil supplies from Iraq at concessionary rates. There was no Jordanian cash payment for this oil either, as it was charged against debt accumulated by Iraq during the Iran–Iraq War. As described earlier, by the late 1980s, Jordan and Iraq had even established fledgling military cooperation, which included a joint training squadron for F-1 Mirage aircraft and Iraqi aerial reconnaissance flights along the Jordan–Israel border.

But the 1990 Iraqi invasion of Kuwait changed the dynamic of relations between Jordan and Iraq. In the late 1980s, Jordan was facing an economic downturn, highlighted by a catastrophic four-month period in 1988 when the Jordanian currency (dinar) lost half of its value.[22] Despite some signs of recovery by 1990, the onset of the Gulf War—with the imposition of economic and trade sanctions on Jordan's leading economic partner—sorely exacerbated the Kingdom's financial difficulties. Jordan's stance during the conflict—preferring an ephemeral "Arab solution" to economic sanctions or military action to liberate Kuwait—prompted several Gulf states to cut their own diplomatic ties with Amman. With the abrupt closure of the Iraqi market and the expulsion of Palestinians (many of whom were Jordanian passport holders) from Kuwait and elsewhere, Jordan lost millions of dollars in customs duties, transport business, and expatriate remittances; in exchange, it gained an increase in unemployment and a flood of refugees.

In the aftermath of the Gulf War, King Hussein struggled to restore the benefits of Jordan's relationship with Iraq while restoring his image as a moderate partner of the West. Criticized in Europe and America for tilting toward Iraq and by Iraq for maintaining neutrality, Jordan emerged from the war politically and economically isolated.[23] As a result, Jordanian relations with both the United States and Iraq suffered significant setbacks. For example, because Jordan remained outside the coalition during the war, U.S. foreign assistance dried up.[24] (See table 1.1.) In the 1980s, U.S. aid had reached $110 million per year; in 1990, it was down to $50 million.[25] Likewise, trade with Iraq—once the driving force of the Jordanian economy—was dramatically limited under the UN-led postwar sanctions regime.

Table 1.1. Annual U.S. Aid to Jordan since the Gulf War ($ in millions)

Fiscal Year (FY)	Economic Support	Food	Military Assistance		Totals
			FMF[a]	IMET[b]	
1991	35.0c	0	20.0[c]	1.3	56.30
1992	30.0[d]	20.0	20.0[d]	0.6	70.60
1993[e]	5.0	30.0	9.0	0.5	44.50
1994[f]	9.0	15.0	9.0	0.8	37.80
1995	7.2	15.0	7.3	1.0	37.20
1996	7.2	21.0	200.0[g]	1.2	237.30
1997[h]	112.2	2.6	30.0	1.7	152.10
1998[h]	150.0	0	75.0[i]	1.6	227.80
1999	150.0	0	70.0[i]	1.6	223.00
1999 (Wye)	50.0	0	50.0	0	100.00
2000	150.0	0	75.0	1.6	228.30
2000 (Wye)	50.0	0	150.0	0	200.00[j]
2001	150.0	0	75.0	1.7	228.40
2002[k]	150.0	0	75.0	1.8	228.20
2003	250.0	0	198.0	2.4	450.40[l]

Adapted from CRS Issue Brief for Congress, "Jordan: U.S. Relations and Bilateral Issues," January 2002, Alfred Prados, Congressional Research Service, Library of Congress.
a. Foreign Military Financing
b. International Military Education and Training Program
c. Suspended in April 1991 under Public Law (P.L.) 102-27: released in early 1993.
d. Released in late July 1993.
e. Restrictions on FY 1993 funds waived by Presidential Determination (PD) 93-39, September 17, 1993.
f. FY1994 funds released by PD 94-11, January 13, 1994, waiving restrictions under P.L. 103-87.
g. Three components: $30 million (administration's original request); $70 million in additional FMF under FY1996 appropriation (P.L. 104-134) to cover balance of F-16 aircraft package; and $100 million in special drawdown authority (P.L. 104-107).
h. These figures include $100 million in economic assistance under the president's Middle East Peace and Stability Fund ($100 million in FY1997, $116 million in FY1998.
i. For each of these two years, FMF figure includes $25 million in drawdown authority.
j. Some of these funds to be obligated in future years (FY2001 or FY2002).
k. Administration's request for FY2002.
l. At the time this book went to press, the administration was considering a large supplemental package to Jordan of approximately $1 billion in ESF/FMF, to include funds to cover eighteen F-16s, over several years.
Note: These figures do not include debt relief subsidy appropriations listed in table 2.1 or small amounts for de-mining assistance.

Despite the fact that the UN Sanctions Committee tolerated Jordan's continued importation of oil from Iraq, the Kingdom initially refused to implement other provisions of the sanctions regime. Under international pressure, in the spring of 1991 the Kingdom did eventually comply (for the most part). (This topic will be discussed in more detail in chapter 3.) After compliance was certified, Japanese and European aid began flowing back into Jordan, and shortly thereafter, relations started to deteriorate with Iraq. While eventually bilateral trade marginally increased, on the diplomatic level ties remained chilly for nearly a decade. In fact the relationship did not register any significant improvement until after King Hussein's death in February 1999.

SWISS BILLS

With minor exceptions, 1993–1999 were rocky years for Jordanian–Iraqi relations. In 1992 and 1993, King Hussein launched a series of well-publicized political liberalizations in the Kingdom. Not surprisingly, this project to "strengthen the democratic experiment" in Jordan—and the king's very public calls for democratization in the Arab world—were not well received either in Iraq or in the Arab sheikhdoms of the Gulf.[26] At about the same time, King Hussein began to criticize the Baghdad leadership—at first implicitly and then more overtly—and initiated contacts with members of the Iraqi opposition.

In May 1993, in what is generally viewed as an act of Iraqi retaliation against Jordan, Baghdad canceled the twenty-five-dinar banknote, known as the "Swiss Bill." Produced abroad, the note was known for its quality, particularly when compared to the domestically minted Iraqi fifty-dinar bill. The Swiss Bill was the currency utilized by Iraqis in their trade with Jordan as well as with the Persian Gulf states.

In late April during a visit to Amman, only a few weeks before the bill was canceled, the Iraqi minister of trade announced that Baghdad had no intention of changing its currency and that the value of the dinar would "increase."[27] The minister's reassuring statements encouraged Jordanian speculation in the twenty-five-dinar bill.[28] Then, after the bill was canceled, the Iraqi border was closed for six days allowing Iraqis—but not foreigners—to exchange the cancelled currency for other Iraqi government notes. The result was that Jordanian businessmen involved in Iraqi trade lost an estimated $250 million in the scramble.

The Iraqi government maintained that the cancellation of the bills was intended to hurt its rebellious Kurdish population and Saddam's enemies in the Gulf. Other reports suggest that the move may have been a countermeasure by the Iraqi government against a CIA attempt to topple Saddam by flooding

Iraq with forged dinar notes.[29] Whatever the official rationale, Jordanians were among the principal victims of this fiscal legerdemain.

In the wake of the currency cancellation, Jordanians were furious. Many were said to have thrown stacks of the bills from their office windows in Amman or to have used the bills as fire kindling. Six Jordanians committed suicide in the days after the affair. Pictures of Saddam, which had been hoisted on placards at pro-Iraq demonstrations only two years earlier, were burned.

THE WADI ARAVA PEACE TREATY

In October 1994, Jordan and Israel signed a historic peace treaty, ending the formal state of war along Israel's longest border and committing themselves to a peace that had the promise of setting new benchmarks for warmth and cooperation. Although it seems almost counterintuitive, Iraq did not actively try to prevent the establishment of a Jordan–Israel peace. Indeed, had Saddam so chosen, according to then Jordanian prime minister Abdel Salam Majali, Iraq "could have damaged the process"[30] and scuttled the accord. But Saddam chose not to. According to Majali, this was a purely pragmatic decision, for at the time, Jordan was Iraq's only window to the outside world.

But even as Iraq was exhibiting restraint as its longtime ally was making peace with Israel, the leadership in Jordan was starting to express criticism of the regime in Baghdad. While hosting Israeli prime minister Yitzhak Rabin in Amman in August 1994, King Hussein made a number of statements to the press criticizing the ongoing provocations of Saddam. Expressing "disappointment" with the Iraqi leader, King Hussein warned that Iraq could be "repeating something that happened four years ago [i.e., the Gulf War]."[31] In subsequent years, Iraq became less muted in its condemnation of aspects of Jordanian policy. In 1996, for example, Iraq's Umm al Ma'arik (Mother of all Battles) radio station accused the Jordanian government of signing "a peace treaty with the Zionist enemy against the will of the people."[32]

At about the same time Jordan signed its treaty with Israel, an odd story began receiving coverage in the press. The reports, which varied in detail, suggested that King Hussein was brokering a deal between the United States and Iraq in which Iraq would be "pardoned" and sanctions lifted if Baghdad would participate in the Arab–Israeli peace process.[33] Although this story appears colored by the residual euphoria of the Gulf War and the optimism of the ongoing post-Madrid negotiations between the Israelis and the Syrians and Palestinians, there is some indication that it had more than a kernel of truth.[34] At the very least, it highlights Jordan's role as mediator and at times speaker for Iraq.

Jordan's treaty with Israel and King Hussein's fledgling criticism of Saddam were accompanied by subtle hints that Jordan might reorient its economy
to become less dependent on Iraq. As then minister of state for parliamentary
affairs Jawad Anani said in September 1994, Jordan "need[s] to restructure to
rebuild ourselves, and bring ourselves into a new set of relations, on mutual
respect and economic interests."[35]

Nine months after Anani's comment, Jordanian–Iraqi ties reached their
lowest point since 1958, with the defection of Hussein Kamel to Jordan trig-
gering a temporary political reorientation of the Kingdom against the regime
in Baghdad.

THE HUSSEIN KAMEL AFFAIR

The June 1995 defection of Hussein Kamel, Saddam's son-in-law and chief
of Iraq's weapons of mass destruction (WMD) programs, signaled the beginning of an overt rift in Jordanian–Iraqi relations that would last nearly
three years. The defection was particularly embarrassing for the regime in
Baghdad. Not only did Kamel have the audacity to flee to Jordan with Saddam's daughter and his WMD secrets, he also brought with him bank accounts worth—according to some estimates—in excess of a billion dollars.
In Amman, Kamel was hosted by King Hussein, who was only too pleased
to use the opportunity to smooth his return into the good graces of the U.S.
government.

With the arrival of Kamel, Jordanian rhetoric and policy took a profound
turn against Iraq. Just two months later, on August 23, 1995, King Hussein
gave a television address to the people of Jordan in which he called for the removal of Saddam. He suggested, via repeated allusions to the period of
Hashemite rule in Iraq, that it might be appropriate for the Hashemites to return to that country. Saying he was "shocked" at what he discovered from his
discussions with Kamel, the king declared: "We must do the impossible and
use all means to rescue Iraq and the Iraqi people."[36] As the king described it:

> Recently, a picture became clear to me reflecting the depth of a different kind of
> suffering [not related to the UN sanctions regime] that seeks to end the Iraqi hu-
> man being's many human rights, a suffering that affected me because of my con-
> cern for those people and my interest in saving them and seeing that they get
> what they are entitled to.[37]

During the months that followed, King Hussein pursued a different type of
discourse harkening back to the days of Iraq's Hashemite rule—a discourse
that represented a distinct change in policy for the Kingdom. The new policy,

at least rhetorically, was geared toward engineering regime change in Bagh-dad. A main weapon in the king's arsenal against Saddam was the common history shared by the two countries—a history that the king believed would resonate among the Jordanian and Iraqi peoples.

As spelled out by King Hussein, this history emphasized three key ele-ments: the transcendent role of Hashemite lineage; the importance of Hashemite leadership in the Great Arab Revolt from 1916 to 1920; and the role the Hashemite monarchy played in Iraq from 1920 to 1958. Taken as a whole, the king's message was that perhaps the same Hashemite family that played such a noble role in Iraq's past could play a role in redeeming Iraq's future.

Indeed, in 1995 and 1996, King Hussein spoke frequently about the fact that he "was the second person after the late King Faysal."[38] Hussein was—technically, at least—Faisal II's heir after the Ba'thists assassinated the latter in July 1958. (Only Britain's lack of enthusiasm for Jordanian military ad-venture kept Hussein from sending his troops into Iraq to avenge the murder and lay claim to the throne.) Hussein also served as deputy head of the short-lived Iraq–Jordan Arab Federation, established as the royalists' response to the Egypt–Syria United Arab Republic. Citing the deep ethnic cleavages among Iraq's Sunni, Shi'ite, and Kurdish communities that were growing more divisive under Ba'thist rule, King Hussein underscored the role of the Hashemites as leaders of Ahl al-Bayt, the Muslim nobility predating ethnic and religious schisms. Speaking of the period following Faisal's deposition, King Hussein said: "We had hoped that the Sunnis, Shi'ites, Arabs, Kurds, and all elements of its [Iraq's] national fabric that the Hashemites had held to-gether would not be torn apart."[39] The message was clear: the Hashemite role, according to the king, was to "try to heal all wounds."[40]

Still, King Hussein was oblique as to a possible future Hashemite role in Iraq. In September 1995, when asked whether the Hashemites would be will-ing to once again "shoulder the responsibility" in Iraq, the king responded: "That is up to the Iraqis themselves. If they found that a particular regime served them in the past or that a certain leadership resolved their differences and achieved their unity, that is up to them."[41]

KING HUSSEIN AND THE IRAQI OPPOSITION

King Hussein began to take an active role in promoting regime change in Iraq. Indeed, both the king and his brother, Prince Hassan bin Talal, began meeting frequently with Iraqi opposition leaders in London and elsewhere.[42] This activity included a critical White House meeting in late 1995 during which King Hussein and Hussein Majd (the Shi'ite leader of the influential

Khoei Foundation) met with President Bill Clinton to determine whether the administration "was serious" about removing Saddam.[43] If the answer was "yes," said the king, then he would be willing to play a more significant role in the fight against Saddam.

It bears mentioning that King Hussein was not alone among Arab leaders in his support for Iraqi opposition groups. Syria, for example, also exhibited sporadic backing, and Iraqi oppositionists were, at times, welcome in Saudi Arabia, Kuwait, and several Persian Gulf countries. The Jordanian role was unique, however, because King Hussein was using his "personal influence on the Iraqi, regional, and international levels and not his country's influence" to try and effect change.[44]

Hussein took several steps in 1995 and 1996 that made his support for Iraqi opposition groups more tangible. Among other actions, he met three times in London with Iraqi National Congress executive chairman Ahmed Chalabi.[45] Likewise, in December 1995, the king offered to host a conference in Jordan for the leadership of the Iraqi opposition. By 1996, not only was the Jordanian government providing sanctuary for Iraqi defectors, but it was stepping up the rhetorical challenge to Saddam's regime.[46] In an interview in the Jordanian daily *al-Dustur* in January 1996, then foreign minister Abdel Karim al-Kabariti called for a new government in Baghdad as the best means for maintaining the territorial integrity and the unity of the Iraqi people. "This can be accomplished" he said, "only through arriving at a constitutional and democratic form [of government] that takes into consideration and observes the pluralism that exists in Iraq."[47]

While the Jordanian government made statements that seemed to suggest receptivity to regime change, the operational details of dealing with the opposition were left to Jordan's intelligence chief, Samih Buttikhi. Under Buttikhi, the cornerstone of the Kingdom's effort against Saddam was the CIA-backed Iraqi National Accord (INA). In February 1996, at the behest of the CIA, Jordan allowed the INA to open a "political" office in Amman. From that point on, this office became a focal point of CIA efforts in Jordan to target Saddam's regime.

Over the past decade, the INA has had several tasks. These have included preparing radio programs to be broadcast into Iraq; serving as an information clearinghouse about Iraq; and acting as intelligence "spotters" for the CIA, providing a steady stream of defectors to be debriefed and possibly reinserted back into Iraq. Primarily, though, the INA office in 1996 was being used as "cover" for preparations for a CIA-led coup in Baghdad. These efforts led only to failure.

According to a variety of reports, the CIA-backed plan centered around a retired officer from the Iraqi Special Forces helicopter unit and his three sons, all officers in Saddam's Republican Guards.[48] But the INA-led scheme—indeed the INA itself—was deeply penetrated by Baghdad, and the plan never fully developed. As was later confirmed, Saddam had learned of the plot more than six months earlier.[49] By mid-June 1996, a series of arrests began in Baghdad, with more than one hundred officers eventually arrested on suspicion of involvement in the plot. Within weeks, several dozen were executed.[50] The aborted coup was an embarrassment to both Washington and Amman.

IRAQ STRIKES BACK, MAYBE

Less than a year after Abdel Karim al-Kabariti was appointed Jordan's prime minister, the Jordanian government agreed to slash price supports on bread in line with an International Monetary Fund economic reform plan. Almost immediately, Jordanians responded angrily to the effective doubling of the price of this basic commodity with three days of violent rioting focused in the poorer regions of south Jordan, most notably in Kerak. While many observers blamed the demonstrations on the absence of any clear "peace dividend" from Jordan's two-year-old treaty with Israel, King Hussein attributed the violence to "foreign circles"—a code for Iraq. It remains unclear exactly what role, if any, Iraq played in fomenting the unrest. Fourteen of those arrested for incitement were members of the Iraq-affiliated Arab Socialist Ba'th Party. Not surprisingly, Khalil Haddadeen, the party's only member in Jordan's lower house of parliament, denied any party connection to the demonstrations.

There is some evidence to suggest that the impetus for the rioting was not Iraq but another of Jordan's neighbors, Saudi Arabia. According to some reports, a favorite chant of protestors in the southern town of Ma'an was "*La lil Hassan wal Hussein, naam lil Khadam al Haramain*"—"No to Hassan and Hussein, Yes to the Servants of Mecca and Medina," a reference to the Saudi ruling family. A Saudi connection would not have been surprising, given the close social, cultural, financial, and clan connections between southern Jordanian tribes and the Saudis.

When Abdel Salam Majali replaced Kabariti as premier in March 1997, relations with Iraq remained chilly but began a gradual thaw. That December, Saddam executed four Jordanians in Baghdad accused of smuggling eight hundred dollars worth of spare automobile parts into Iraq. Jordanian officials protested the executions, with King Hussein denouncing the killings as "a heinous crime" and warning that Jordan would "not forgive any party that considers [Jordanian blood] cheap or spills it."[51] Some days later, however,

Majali tried to place the executions in context of the overall bilateral relationship. "I cannot imagine," he said, "that this incident will have a major impact on the economic situation." He then explained that Jordan had its own strategy to deal with "major and minor" events in Jordanian–Iraqi relations. Given the economic imperative of the relationship, it appears that Jordan chose not to consider this unfortunate incident a "major event."

STATUS OF BILATERAL RELATIONS AT THE END OF KING HUSSEIN'S REIGN: OPERATION DESERT FOX

Although Jordan and Iraq arrived at a mild political detente in 1997–1998, during those years the Kingdom maintained what could be described as a see-saw pattern of both disdain for the Iraqi regime and sympathy for the Iraqi people. These tenuous relations were once again tested in December 1998, when the United States and Britain launched Operation Desert Fox, a four-day air campaign against Iraq, to compel Saddam Hussein to comply with UN resolutions on inspections of his WMD and ballistic missile programs.

During the buildup to Operation Desert Fox, King Hussein was in Minnesota, receiving treatment for cancer. During a visit to the United States the previous March, the king had met with Iraqi opposition leader Ahmed Chalabi to discuss strategies for how to remove Saddam. The king also held meetings with President Clinton and Secretary of State Madeleine Albright during this visit. It was alleged that the king carried with him a letter from Iraqi deputy vice president Tariq Aziz, while still other reports indicated that the king presented a memo to Clinton regarding the dangers that Iraq posed to Jordan. To the king's chagrin, the United States evidently indicated no interest in either reaching an accommodation with or taking action against Iraq to relieve pressure on Jordan.[52]

As the crisis over inspections developed during the summer and autumn of 1998, Jordan adopted what it considered to be a principled and neutral position, just as it did in 1990. The Jordanian stance had three main points. First, Jordan maintained that international legitimacy should be applied "across the board," that is, UN resolutions on Israel and the Palestinians should be enforced with the same sense of urgency as were resolutions on Iraq. Second, Jordan called for dialogue with Iraq, rather than reliance on military force. Third, Jordan formally called on Iraq to comply with UN resolutions.[53]

Fearing a replay of the destabilizing spillover that accompanied the 1991 Gulf War, Jordan braced for the U.S.-led air strikes. Jordanian regent Prince Hassan, for example, expressed the Kingdom's concerns about another mini-war on its border. Primarily, he said, his apprehensions centered around "the possibility of displaced refugees, the breakdown of infrastructure, and the shortage of oil supplies." The prince added, "The sense of deja-vu does not make it any better."[54]

For Jordan, the fear of having to once again accommodate a deluge of Iraqi refugees was disquieting. In 1990, thousands of Iraqis fled Baghdad to seek refuge in Jordan. This time, as a precaution, Jordanian minister of interior Nayef al-Qadi announced that the Kingdom would provide humanitarian support for fleeing Iraqis but only on the Iraqi side of the border; none would be permitted entry into Jordan. Indeed, on December 17—the day after the strikes were initiated—Jordan closed its borders with Iraq to prevent an influx of refugees.

In addition to these external pressures, the Kingdom was feeling pressure from the street. After nearly eight years of sanctions against Iraq, with the concomitant economic implications for Jordan, most Jordanians roundly opposed the official Jordanian position. When the attacks eventually came, not only were Jordanian Islamists and pro-Iraqi intellectuals critical of Jordan's neutral position, but the normally quiescent lower house of parliament actually passed a nonbinding resolution condemning the strikes and demanding an end to Jordan's enforcement of sanctions against Iraq. In response, then minister of information Nasser Judeh issued a statement informing the parliamentarians that Jordanian policy on this issue was not under their jurisdiction, but rather "under the government's responsibility."[55]

The palace reacted to the bombings by calling for restraint on all sides. On December 18, Prince Hassan issued a public appeal for an end to the U.S.-led strikes, and a few days later, while touring the eastern border region, Hassan spoke of the suffering of the "fraternal" Iraqi people and the continued necessity of U.S.–Iraqi dialogue. Yet just a week later, during a December 27 meeting of the Arab Parliamentary Union in Amman to discuss Operation Desert Fox, the prince took a different tack in a speech focusing on the need for democracy in Iraq, and did not even mention the air strikes.[56] Hassan was roundly condemned by Iraqi officials and media.

THE DEATH OF KING HUSSEIN

The ambivalence—if not disdain—with which Saddam viewed King Hussein was clearly exhibited after the latter's death on February 7, 1999. Despite having tried to mediate a peaceful solution to the 1990–1991 Gulf crisis,[57] the king was remembered by the Iraqi regime as the man who had welcomed Saddam's renegade son-in-law and then dared to call for new leadership in Baghdad. Shortly before the king's death, Saddam appealed—via a speech broadcast on al-Jazeera satellite television—to Arabs residing in pro-Western Arab states to overthrow their leaders, whom he described as "stooges, collaborators, throne

dwarfs and cowards." The reference to "throne dwarfs" was widely understood as a reference to King Hussein and Prince Hassan.

When King Hussein died, the evening news on Baghdad television gave
the story a brief mention more than fifteen minutes into the broadcast. A short
article, scarcely a few lines long, appeared in the leading Iraqi daily *Babil*; no
obituary appeared in any Iraqi newspaper. To a funeral that was, arguably, the
most widely attended by world leaders since the death of Winston Churchill,
Iraq sent a low-level delegation headed by a powerless vice president (one of
several in Iraq) and a deputy foreign minister.

Despite these diplomatic slights, Jordan's new king, Abdullah, went out of
his way to make an overture to the Iraqi delegation, telling them that Jordan
was prepared to consider "means of enhancing" economic ties between the
countries.[58] Soon thereafter, a top official in the Iraqi oil ministry reassured
Jordan about Baghdad's policy of supplying Jordan's oil needs and promised
that the 1999 oil protocol signed would remain in force.[59]

CONCLUSION

Because of the closed nature of Iraqi society under Saddam Hussein, it is difficult to ascertain exactly how Iraqis felt about King Hussein's proposal for
regime change and democracy in Iraq. The king's August 23, 1995, television
address—in which he called for the removal of Saddam—was also broadcast
live in Iraq, but little is known about how it was received. Privately, many
members of the Iraqi opposition—be they Shi'ite, Kurdish, or Sunni—appear
to be very favorably inclined toward the Hashemites. One London-based
Shi'ite opposition leader encapsulated what appears to be a consensus position among the many factions of the opposition: "There is definite goodwill
and nostalgia toward the Hashemites in Iraq."[60] Interestingly, these positive
sentiments toward the Hashemites may constitute one of the few areas of consensus for the opposition.[61]

While these sentiments appear to be genuine, it bears noting that Iraqis
were not always so fond of their Hashemite cousins in Jordan. The 1958 cre-
ation of the Iraq–Jordan Arab Federation was given a lukewarm reception
among many in Baghdad who saw it as little more than "a family compact between an unloved and alien royal house"[62] and feared that the price for the
federation was that Iraq would have to assume part of Jordan's chronic financial deficits.

Although these sentiments may be an accurate reflection of what occurred
in the 1950s, it is at least worth considering whether there has been a re-
assessment by Iraqis of their own history. Naturally, after forty years of repressive Ba'th government, Iraqis today see the Hashemite years in a differ-

ent light. As one commentator—albeit with an interest in the restoration of the Hashemite monarchy in Iraq—noted, "Iraqis have good memories of the monarchic era, *especially when compared with the republican era that has followed*. This is why Iraqis are interested in the issue of the return of the monarchy to Iraq."[63] Until there is greater access to Iraq, this question will likely remain unanswerable.

Back in Jordan, however, the popular perception of the historic Hashemite role in Iraq is more accessible. Perhaps not surprisingly, Jordanians of all stripes describe the brief period of Hashemite rule in Iraq as something of a renaissance, followed by years of decline. This view is predominant among members of Jordan's East Banker elite and Bedouin communities, but it is also articulated by Palestinians and Islamists in the Kingdom. As one Jordanian royal confided, "Jordanians have cultural amnesia. The Iraqis have a keen memory that the slippery slope started in 1958."[64]

Interestingly, even some of the most ardent supporters of Saddam in the Kingdom articulate the above view. Noting that even in ancient times Iraq was never a "healthy society," pro-Iraq commentator Tariq Masarweh recognized the positive role the Hashemites once played in Iraq. "In Hashemite times," he said, "they agreed to be Iraqis, not Arabs, not Kurds. They agreed to be Arabs, not Shi'a and Sunni."[65] Today Iraq is a society rife with internal ethnic and tribal cleavages. The difference, according to Masarweh, was Hashemite rule.

These sentiments are echoed by the full spectrum of Jordanian popular opinion. For example, former Islamic Action Front official and minister of administrative development Bassam al-Amoush once claimed that Iraqis "miss the Hashemites."[66] Al-Amoush's assessment was seconded by minister of labor Eid al-Fayez, of Bedouin origin, who maintained that the Iraqi people "still love and admire the Jordanian monarch" despite what happened in 1958. Iraqis believe, he said, that they "made a mistake."[67]

Along a similar line of logic, one former Jordanian minister who traveled frequently to Iraq in the 1990s opined that Iraqis harbor a deep guilt about the slaughter of the Iraqi royals in 1958. Iraqis, he suggested, "cannot accept the fact that they killed the Hashemites." Moreover, he stated, "Some Iraqis believe that this [i.e., Saddam] is their punishment." To illustrate his point, the former minister described a visit he paid to the home of some acquaintances in Baghdad. Under the economic duress of sanctions, the family had been forced to sell most of their prized possessions. They refused, however, to part with some dinner plates bearing the images of assassinated members of the royal family, King Faisal II and Regent Abdu Illah.

While there is no obvious policy implication to these anecdotes, they do reflect a predominant Jordanian mind-set regarding Iraq. Jordanians not only feel close to Iraqis, but, by and large, they also believe that the Hashemites are beloved in Iraq.

NOTES

1. "Honor killings" typically involve male family members murdering a female relative whose alleged immoral sexual behavior has brought "dishonor" on the family. Women subject to execution include those thought to be unfaithful to their husbands and women who have been raped. A family's honor is "redeemed" when the woman is killed. There is a fairly high incidence of "honor killings" in Jordan. Criminal penalties for those who are convicted of honor killings in the Kingdom are lenient.

2. Kamel Abu Jabr, interview by author, detailed notes, Amman, Jordan, October 10, 1999.

3. *King Husayn Addresses Nation on Iraq*, Amman Jordan Television Network, August 23, 1995, cited in Foreign Broadcast Information Service–Near East and South Asia (FBIS-NES-95-164), August 24, 1995.

4. Amman Chamber of Commerce chairman Yanal al-Bustami, interview by author, detailed notes, Amman, Jordan, October 2, 1999.

5. "Jordan's Prince Hassan on Palestinian Issue," *Al-Ahram*, December 3, 1998, cited in FBIS-NES-98-337, December 7, 1998.

6. Khaldoun Abu Hassan, interview by author, detailed notes, Amman, Jordan, October 12, 1999.

7. "Jordan's Prince Hassan on Palestinian Issue," *Al-Ahram*, December 3, 1998, cited in FBIS-NES-98-337, December 7, 1998. Interestingly, in the same interview when asked how he "describe[d] relations between Jordan and Syria," he replied, "I think dialogue with our Syrian brothers is required."

8. *King Husayn Addresses Nation on Iraq*, Amman Jordan Television Network, August 23, 1995, cited in FBIS-NES-95-164, August 24, 1995.

9. *King Husayn Discusses Iraq with Journalists*, Amman Jordan Television Network, September 16, 1995, cited in FBIS-NES-95-180, September 18, 1995.

10. Abdel Salam al-Majali, interview by author, detailed notes, Amman, Jordon, October 3, 1999.

11. Charles Tripp, *A History of Iraq* (Cambridge: Cambridge University Press, 2000).

12. Tripp, *History of Iraq*, 33.

13. Saddam's letter was read at the summit by Izzat Ibrahim, vice chairman of the Iraqi Revolutionary Command Council. See appendix A for an English translation of the full text.

14. Prince Hassan bin Talal, interview by author, detailed notes, London, U.K., July 10, 2000.

15. See *King Husayn Discusses Iraq with Journalists*, Amman Jordan Television Network, September 16, 1995, cited in FBIS-NES-95-180, September 18, 1995. During that speech, he referred to Iraq as "our strategic depth and our brother."

16. Mwrawid al-Tel, interview by author, detailed notes, Amman, Jordan, October 7, 1999.

17. Daniel Dishon, "Inter-Arab Affairs," *Middle East Contemporary Survey 1978–1979* (New York: Holmes & Meier, 1978–1979).

18. Wahab al-Sha'ir, interview by author, detailed notes, Amman, Jordan, July 8, 2000.

19. Aida Dabbas, interview by author, detailed notes, Amman, Jordan, June 28, 2000.

20. *IMF Direction of Trade Statistical Yearbook, 1989*, 243. The total Jordanian exports that year amounted to $788.6 million.

21. Jawad Anani, a former minister of state for prime ministry affairs and chief of the Royal Court describes this shift in the labor force as "Dutch disease."

22. For a more detailed discussion of this period, see Timothy Piro's *The Political Economy of Market Reform in Jordan* (Lanham, Md.: Rowman & Littlefield, 1998).

23. For Jordan's side of the story, see: *The White Paper: Jordan and the Gulf Crisis, August 1990–March 1991*, The Government of the Hashemite Kingdom of Jordan, Amman, August 1991. This book is printed and distributed by the government of Jordan but not available for purchase. It is available in both Arabic and English. Other sources close to King Hussein whisper that the king was personally very happy with Saddam's invasion of Kuwait.

24. Aid was resumed in 1993. Sums rebounded and surpassed their pre–Gulf War levels following the signing of the 1994 Wadi Arava peace treaty between Jordan and Israel.

25. Murray Waas and Doublas Frantz, "Jordan Gave Iraq Broad Assistance," *Los Angeles Times*, November 29, 1992.

26. See, for example, Jamal Halaby, "Jordan's King Urges Democracy in the Arab World," Associated Press, April 5, 1993.

27. "Jordanian Columnist: Ban the Iraqi Dinar," *Mideast Mirror*, May 7, 1993.

28. Randa Habib, interview by author, detailed notes, Amman, Jordan, October 2, 2000.

29. Paul Lewis, "Iraq Food Imports Are Said to Drop," *New York Times*, August 4, 1992.

30. Abdel Salam Majali, interview by author, detailed notes, Amman, Jordan, October 3, 2000.

31. Richard Beeston, "Rabin Visit Confirms Husain Rift with Saddam," *The Times*, October 14, 1994. Hussein was probably referring to statements made by Saddam during the early part of 1994, in which he threatened both the United States and the Gulf states. In retrospect, Hussein's comments to the press were apocryphal. On October 7, 1994, Saddam mobilized some sixty thousand Republican Guards for a faux march toward Kuwait. For more details on this episode, see Laurie Mylroie, *Study of Revenge: Saddam's Unfinished War against America* (Washington, D.C.: AEI Press, 2000).

32. Natasha al-Bukhari, "Officials Say Ties with Iraq Not to Suffer Due to Riots," *Jordan Times*, August 21, 1996.

33. See, for example, "King Hussein Does Not Rule Out Baghdad's Eventual Involvement in Mideast Peace Moves," *Mideast Mirror*, August 18, 1994.

34. See, for example "Iraq to Make Deal with Israel," August 11, 1994, and "Jordan Briefs Iraq on Peace Developments," August 14, 1994, Xinhua News Agency.

35. Jawad Anani, speech before the Middle East Policy Council, September 1996.

36. *King Husayn Discusses Iraq, Regional Issues,* Amman Radio Jordan Network, September 7, 1995, cited in FBIS-NES-95-174, September 8, 1995.

37. *King Husayn Discusses Iraq, Regional Issues,* Amman Radio Jordan Network, September 7, 1995, cited in FBIS-NES-95-174, September 8, 1995.

38. *King Husayn Interviewed on Iraq, Peace Process,* Amman Jordan Television Network, September 26, 1995, cited in FBIS-NES-95-187, September 26, 1995.

39. *King Husayn Address Nation on Iraq,* Amman Jordan Television Network, August 23, 1995, cited in FBIS-NES-95-164, August 24, 1995.

40. "Text of King Husayn Al-Qabas Interview," *Al-Aswaq,* February 25, 1996, cited in FBIS-NES-96-038, February 26, 1996.

41. *King Husayn Discusses Iraq, Regional Issues,* Amman Radio Jordan Network, September 7, 1995, cited in FBIS-NES-95-174, September 8, 1995.

42. The authoritative account of Hashemite ties with the Iraqi opposition is in David Wurmser, *Tyranny's Ally: America's Failure to Defeat Saddam Hussein* (Washington, D.C.: AEI Press, 1999).

43. Laith Kubba, interview by author, detailed notes, Washington, D.C., August 25, 2000. Kubba was an employee of the Khoei Foundation at the time and attended the meetings in Washington, D.C.

44. "Ahmed Chalabi in an Interview with the Lebanese Newspaper *Al-Safir* about the Jordanian Undertaking," in *Al-Malaf al-Iraqi (The Iraqi File),* no. 50, February 1995.

45. Ahmed Chalabi, interview by author, July 2001. King Hussein met Chalabi in Washington, D.C., in 1998 as well.

46. Hussein Kamel and his brother returned to Iraq on their own volition on February 20, 1995, and were promptly killed. Even so, the Jordanian policy of providing sanctuary continued. One month after Kamel returned to Iraq, the Kingdom provided asylum to Nazar Khazraji, a former chief of staff of the Iraqi army.

47. "Al-Kabariti Interviewed on Israel, Syria, Iraq," *Al-Dustur,* January 4, 1996, cited in FBIS-NES-96-004, January 10, 1996.

48. Andrew Cockburn and Patrick Cockburn, *Out of the Ashes: The Resurrection of Saddam Hussein* (New York: HarperCollins, 1999), 223.

49. Iraqi National Congress president Ahmed Chalabi had informed the CIA of the breech in secrecy nearly three months earlier, but the agency decided to nevertheless push forward with the ill-fated plan.

50. See Wurmser, *Tyranny's Ally,* 25.

51. "Iraqi Envoy Confirms Jordanian Not to Be Executed," *Jordan Times,* December 14, 1997, cited in FBIS-NES-97-348, December 16, 1997.

52. According to sources close to the Royal Court, there was little interest in this subject. During an earlier meeting on April 2, 1997, King Hussein was said to have brought up the topic with Secretary of State Albright, but time was limited as Albright was scheduled to toss out the first pitch at opening day of the Baltimore Orioles baseball season in Camden Yards. The king, it is said, was livid.

53. Nasser Judeh, then secretary of information, government of Jordan, interview by author, detailed notes, Amman, Jordan, October 10, 2000.

54. Ghalia Alul, "Crown Prince Hasan: Time Running Out for Iraq," *Jordan Times*, February 11, 1998, cited in FBIS-NES-98-042, February 12, 1998.

55. Caroline Faraj, "Government Reply to Call for Lifting Embargo Unclear," *Jordan Times*, December 24–25, 1998, cited in FBIS-NES-98-358, December 28, 1998.

56. "Arab Leaders Row over Iraq as They Await the Next US Assault," *Mideast Mirror*, January 4, 1999.

57. See *The White Paper: Jordan and the Gulf Crisis, August 1990–March 1991*, The Government of the Hashemite Kingdom of Jordan, Amman, August 1991. This book is printed and distributed by the government of Jordan but not available for purchase. It is available in both Arabic and English. King Hussein met with Saddam in Baghdad no less than five times between July 1990 and March 1991.

58. Douglas Jehl, "Jordanians Pay Tribute to Late King and His Heir," *New York Times*, February 10, 1999, sec. A, 8.

59. "Baghdad: sanuwasil amdad al-Urdun bijamia ihtijajatahu al-niftiyya," *Al-Dustur*, February 11, 1999.

60. Ghassan Attiyeh, interview by author, detailed notes, London, U.K., July 10, 2000.

61. To the Sunni tribes, a Hashemite return is appealing because it might prevent the type of violent retribution that could accompany regime change. Moreover, it would prevent a Shi'ite-Kurdish federation aimed at the isolation of the Sunni heartland. Kurds, too, recognize the inherent benefit that the Hashemites would afford a post-Saddam Iraq. As one KDP leader confided, not only are they religiously acceptable, they could also provide the societal glue necessary to keep Iraq unified. Finally, perhaps the leading advocates among the Iraqi opposition for a Hashemite restoration would be the Shi'ites. For the Shi'a of Iraq, the Hashemites are Ahl al-Bayt—revered as relatives of the Prophet Muhammed. Given their lineage, even though they are Sunni Muslims, they are said to maintain the status of "Imam" among the Shi'a. During his lifetime, King Hussein cultivated personal relationships with Abu al-Qasim al-Khoe'i and his son Abdel Majid al-Khoe'i—leaders of Iraq's Shi'ite community. In the early 1990s, Abu al-Qasim al-Khoe'i was said to have issued a *fatwa* (religious edict) supporting King Hussein's legitimate right as heir to the throne of Iraq.

62. Uriel Dann, *Iraq under Qassem* (New York: Preager, 1969).

63. "Hashemite al-Sharif Bin Husayn Interviewed," *Al-Majallah*, January 7, 1996, cited in FBIS-NES-96-064, April 2, 1996. Emphasis added.

64. Interview with a Hashemite royal.

65. Tariq Masarweh, interview by author, detailed notes, Amman, Jordan, October 11, 1999.

66. Bassam al-Amoush, interview by author, detailed notes, Amman, Jordan, October 9, 1999.

67. Eid al-Fayez, interview by author, detailed notes, Amman, Jordan, October 2, 1999.

Chapter Two

Economics

THE INTERPLAY BETWEEN POLITICS AND ECONOMICS

Jordanians often describe their relationship with Iraq as a type of symbiosis. Iraq, they say, needs the "Jordanian lung." This is most important in terms of economics.

The deep economic bonds between Amman and Baghdad represent a relatively new phenomenon. For much of history, the people and the lands east of the Jordan River were oriented westward. Socially and culturally, towns in Transjordan—from Irbid to Kerak—were more closely related to sister cities in Palestine, from Haifa and Acre in the north to Hebron and Jerusalem in the south, than they were in a north-south axis inside Transjordan itself. Financially and economically, Jordan looked westward as well, both for trade with the Mediterranean coast and for financial aid from Western powers, first Britain and then the United States. All this changed in the 1980s, with King Hussein's severance of "legal and administrative" links with the West Bank; the reemergence of a "Jordanian-first" approach in response to the Israeli Likud Party's "Jordan is Palestine" rhetoric, the first Palestinian uprising in 1988–1990, and, most importantly, the bust of the oil boom, which dried up sources of Arab aid and remittances of Jordanian workers abroad. These factors left Iraq as Jordan's main partner for trade and lone, consistent source for economic assistance. The fact that Amman and Baghdad both viewed the Iranian revolution in the same light—that is, as a direct threat to the Sunni Arab lands of the Mashreq—cemented the special connection.

In economic terms, the result was Jordan's abject dependence on Iraq. During the nearly decade-long Iran–Iraq War, with the Shatt al-Arab shipping lane closed to civilian traffic, Iraq cultivated Jordan as its lead supplier and primary transit route for material. Bereft of options for a steady source of foreign currency, Jordan readily obliged. Factories were constructed, roads were built, a substantial trucking industry was developed, and the port of Aqaba was modernized, all to serve the war economy of Iraq. By the mid-1980s, Jordan had emerged as the entrepôt to Iraq. When the Iran–Iraq War ended in 1988, bilateral trade between the states had reached almost $1 billion a year.

For Jordan, Iraq was an economic godsend. A small, poor country with few natural resources, Jordan's own market of 5 million people was too small to justify significant investment in factories, ports, and other infrastructure. But serving as lead supplier to Iraq, a wealthy state with extensive oil reserves and a population of about 20 million, gave massive investment a sound rationale. Thanks to Iraq (and the war with Iran), Jordan enjoyed relatively booming years in the late 1980s.

But the Iraqi invasion of Kuwait in August 1990 changed everything. While Amman initially sought to maintain its trade relations with Baghdad despite the imposition of UN sanctions, international pressure mounted, and the Kingdom was eventually compelled to adhere to the sanctions regime. The result was the crippling of the Jordanian economy overnight. Aqaba port lay empty, thousands of trucks that used to ply the Aqaba–Baghdad route sat idle in desert truck farms, hundreds of construction projects funded through the proceeds of Jordan–Iraq trade were put on hold. While Jordan did enjoy a brief construction boom—fueled by the thousands of Palestinians who returned to Amman, Zarq, and Irbid and built homes with their Persian Gulf–based earnings—this was a fleeting mirage. After several years, the magnitude of Jordan's desperate situation became clear. Indeed, it is widely acknowledged today that Jordan is second only to Iraq as the country whose economy was most hurt by the imposition of UN sanctions.

The impact of sanctions on Jordan did not go unnoticed. The UN, for example, took the extraordinary step of making an exception to the sanctions regime for Iraqi oil exports that were the Kingdom's only ensured source of energy. This permitted Jordan to purchase oil from Iraq at preferential prices, the core of the special economic relationship between the two countries. Given that the United States and Arab countries had effectively cut off Jordan because of its neutralist approach to the Iraq–Kuwait conflict, Jordan was forced to rely on Saddam more than ever. As former Jordanian prime minister Abdel Salam Majali put it succinctly, "Saddam came to our rescue."[1]

The result was a deepening of Jordan's already unhealthy dependence on Iraq and the whims of its unpredictable dictator. With the huge (by Jordanian standards) Iraqi market seemingly so secure, Jordanian entrepreneurs refused to take risks elsewhere. Few wanted to earn the wrath of the Iraqis by testing the trade waters with Israel, for example. Even during the difficult early days of the sanctions in the mid- to late 1990s, many Jordanian businessmen preferred to keep their ties to Iraq so they could, in the words of former Jordanian minister of trade and industry Muhammed Asfour, "be in a stronger position when the sanctions end."[2] After two decades of drinking solely at the Iraqi trough, as of 2002 the Jordanian economy remained inextricably linked to Iraq, with Jordanian entrepreneurs having little indigenous initiative to diversify or modify their orientation. This has left the Kingdom vulnerable to Saddam's machinations and manipulations.

The balance of this chapter discusses the economic factors that underlie the Jordanian–Iraqi relationship. This is a story about trade and aid, about state-to-state protocols, and about Iraqi largesse. It is also a story about the process of trade, that is, transport, and its strategic implications in terms of enforcing or busting UN sanctions on Iraq. In addition, this chapter will explore the factors that encourage Amman's economic ties with Baghdad, often to the exclusion of other alternatives.

HOW JORDANIAN–IRAQI TRADE WORKS

Since the late 1990s, most of the trade between Jordan and Iraq has occurred under the auspices of bilateral oil and trade protocols. Every year Amman and Baghdad negotiate an agreement to define how much oil Iraq will provide to Jordan and how much the Kingdom will "pay" in return. Jordan does not actually pay for the oil in cash; instead, Amman and Baghdad have established a barter arrangement incorporated into a trade protocol negotiated alongside the oil protocol. Commodities subject to this agreement normally include construction materials, metal furniture, detergents, electrical panels, and pipes.

In addition to the system of protocols that regulate much of the bilateral trade, Jordan exports goods to Iraq via the UN-sponsored Oil-for-Food program. Within this framework, established in 1996, Jordanian tenders compete with tenders from numerous other countries to win contracts to supply Iraq with foodstuffs and medicines. A successful contractor supplies the goods directly to Iraq and receives payment from a UN-controlled bank account in Paris funded from the proceeds of Iraqi oil sales.

OIL AND AID

Oil is the lubricant of Jordan's relations with Iraq.[3] Iraq provides Jordan with its total annual needs of crude oil and oil derivatives at a low price. Indeed, the difference between the world market price and the price Jordan pays is a sum that far surpasses any other source of aid Jordan receives. The result: Iraq has been, for many years, Jordan's greatest source of foreign aid.

The Jordanian–Iraqi oil arrangement today is largely the product of the Iran–Iraq War, which lasted from 1980 to 1988. At the beginning of the 1980s, Jordan received most of its oil from Saudi Arabia. In fact, Amman and Riyadh signed an accord in 1983 committing the latter to provide Jordan with its total annual supply of crude through 1985. While Jordan paid for this oil, Saudi Arabia reportedly also provided a package of several million dollars to King Hussein.[4] Developments in Iraq, however, gave the Jordanians an opportunity to negotiate an even better deal with Baghdad.

Wartime Iraq needed Jordan as a safe and consistent source of materiel, but by 1982, Baghdad could no longer afford to pay in cash for all of its military and civilian needs. When Iraq curtailed its imports from Jordan due to the economic crunch, Amman extended export credits to Baghdad. This gave a huge boost to Jordanian exports to Iraq, so much so that by the mid-1980s, Iraq was absorbing nearly one-third of all Jordanian exports. At the same time, though, Iraq was accruing a significant amount of debt to Jordan. To address this problem, Jordan and Iraq initiated a barter arrangement in 1984 in which Iraq provided ten thousand barrels of oil per day to the Kingdom in exchange for goods and services.[5] In 1985 when the agreement with Saudi Arabia expired, Iraq became Jordan's leading supplier of oil. Jordan then enjoyed several boom years, with the Kingdom's economy fueled by Iraq's wartime needs. But when the Iraq–Iran War ended three years later, Jordanian–Iraqi trade slowed.

Already suffering from recession, Jordan's economy was dealt a terrible shock by Iraq's invasion of Kuwait and the subsequent imposition of UN sanctions coupled with the cutoff of Iraqi oil, aid from Persian Gulf countries, and remittances from Jordanian Palestinian workers formerly residing in Gulf countries. Closed off from markets to the south (Gulf), north (due to frigid relations with Assad's Syria), and west (due to the Palestinian uprising), Jordan had few options but to turn back to the east—Iraq—for its economic survival.

During the final years of King Hussein's reign, economic dealings between Jordan and Iraq experienced dramatic volatility. Variations in the annual protocol occurred in part due to fluctuations in the global oil market. To a certain extent, Jordan determines how large or small the trade protocol will be based on a rough calculation of what the market price of oil will be during the coming year. For example, when oil prices declined in the mid-1990s, Jordan was compelled to decrease the value of its trade protocol with Iraq.

As much as oil prices and economic rationale influenced decision making, however, it seems that politics were primarily responsible for the trade protocol variations. When, in 1995, the king decided to cast Jordan's lot with those favoring a "regime change" in Baghdad, Saddam likewise slashed trade with the Kingdom. All these factors influenced the price per barrel Saddam's Iraq

Table 2.1. Value of Jordanian–Iraqi Protocols, 1995–2001

	1995	1996	1997	1998	1999	2000	2001
Price per Barrel		$15.25	$19.10	$16.10	$13.50	$19.00	$20.90
Trade Protocol (in $millions)	$400	$220	$255	$255	$200	$250	$450

Note: In 1998, oil prices declined and Jordan eventually paid $8.40 per barrel.

was paid for supplying oil to Jordan. As table 2.1 indicates, the key issue for Jordan in recent years is less the assurance of supply than the volatility of price.

THE 2000 OIL AND TRADE PROTOCOLS

Unlike the 2001 protocol negotiations that were completed in just about one month, negotiations for the 2000 Jordanian–Iraqi oil protocol were long and drawn out, characterized throughout by tension and, at times, hostility. Details of the negotiations provide insight into how the protocol system works. In fact, the discussions about oil were not really negotiations—if negotiations connote bargaining. Rather, the talks appeared to be an exercise in persuasion, with Jordan using all means at its disposal to elicit from Iraq the largest feasible financial aid package.

Former minister of trade and industry Muhammed Asfour was—at least for the initial phase of the 2000 protocol discussions—the leading Jordanian representative in charge of negotiations. According to Asfour, the Iraqis were tough negotiators, exacerbated by the fact that the Jordanians themselves had little leverage. Iraq wanted a larger trade protocol, but given financial constraints imposed by Jordan's Central Bank, Jordanian negotiators had limited flexibility to increase the protocol. Given these parameters, the Jordanian delegation possessed no way to wrest a better offer from their Iraqi counterparts. This proved especially problematic for the Jordanians, as the Iraqis at first demanded a price per barrel of $19—$5.50 more than the 1999 per barrel price of $13.50.

One tactic employed by Asfour to strengthen his delegations' negotiating hand and compel a more reasonable offer was to suggest that if the Iraqis would not cut a better deal, Jordan would get its oil supplies from Saudi Arabia.[6] Clearly, however, the Iraqis were not threatened by Asfour's ploy and did not budge from their position. Of course, the Iraqis were correct in their assumption that Jordan had no contingency plan. As Jordan's energy minister later admitted, the Kingdom had no plans to "search for alternative petroleum sources."[7] This was particularly the case, he added, after the United States failed to persuade Saudi Arabia to fill the void.

In retrospect, Jordan's problems with Iraq in the course of the 2000 trade protocol negotiations were due in part to policy differences. In his first year on the throne, Jordan's new king Abdullah invested considerable effort in repairing Jordan's ties with the Persian Gulf, particularly with Kuwait and Saudi Arabia. While these efforts did not succeed in winning commitments of alternative oil supplies at concessionary prices, they did reopen some dormant trade ties and start discussions about Jordanian expatriates returning to work in the Gulf. None of this was welcome news in Baghdad.

In addition, it appears that some of Jordan's negotiating difficulties were related to personality problems. Apparently, the Iraqis felt that the Jordanian trade minister was not deferential enough in his approach. An exchange between Asfour and Iraqi oil minister Amir Rasheed is illustrative. During the October 1999 Baghdad International Trade Fair, just after the protocol negotiations commenced, Rasheed asked Asfour what he would do if Iraq stopped giving Jordan oil. Asfour boldly—and rashly—replied by asking Rasheed what Iraq would do if Jordan closed its borders.[8] If this exchange is any indication of the overall tenor of top-level interactions, it is little wonder that the two sides had made little progress by December.

Jordanian–Iraqi negotiations were at an impasse. There were no signs that Iraq would be forthcoming with a more lucrative offer. At the same time, Jordanian officials were starting to speak publicly about the economic hardship that $19 per barrel would precipitate. Realistically, they argued, to keep the budget deficit at a manageable level, the Kingdom could not afford to pay more than $15.

Four months into the negotiations, Asfour was sacked and replaced with his deputy, Muhammed Halayqa, a longtime ministry technocrat. Asfour's removal sparked speculation in Jordan and the pan-Arab press that Iraqi officials had demanded the ouster. While this explanation seems plausible, especially given the centrality of the oil deal to the Jordanian economy, the charge was never substantiated.

In the wake of Asfour's departure, King Abdullah dispatched foreign minister Abdul Ilah al-Khatib to Baghdad to get negotiations back on track. According to reports, while in Baghdad, Khatib informed Iraqi officials that the Kingdom "cannot bear any unreasonable increase" in the oil bill.[9] At $19 per barrel, it was calculated that the tab for Jordan would amount to an additional $170–$180 million, a sum that would effectively break Jordan's bank. Nevertheless, the Iraqis were apparently unmoved and rebuffed Khatib's efforts to lobby for a better offer.

On January 21, 2000, a Jordanian delegation headed by new minister of trade and industry Muhammed Halayqa departed for Baghdad. After two days of meetings, the protocols were signed on January 22. The terms of the protocols,

Table 2.2.   2000 Oil Protocol Work Sheet

4.8 million tons of oil = 98,000 barrels per day
@ $9.50 per barrel (compared to then global market price of $31.00 per barrel).
Discount equates to $22.50 per barrel.

$22.50 × 98,000 barrels = $805 million.

As payment for this $805 million, Jordan sends $200 million worth of products to Iraq.

The Iraqi oil grant to Jordan hence amounted to $605 million.

while viewed as favorable toward Jordan, were not as generous as officials had hoped. In the end, Jordan agreed to pay a maximum of $19 per barrel for 2.4 million tons of oil, while the remaining 2.4 million tons (for a total of 4.8 million) were provided free of charge. In exchange, Jordan increased the trade protocol to $300 million, of which $50 million would be applied toward the Iraqi debt to Jordan. (See table 2.2 for an oil protocol work sheet.)

THE 2001 OIL AND TRADE PROTOCOLS

Terms of the 2001 agreements—which were signed in the aftermath of several conciliatory Jordanian political gestures toward Iraq in 2000—are widely viewed as being among the most beneficial the Kingdom has ever received.[10] Compared with prior Jordanian–Iraqi pacts, negotiations for the 2001 protocol were not especially contentious. Discussions were initiated in October and were finalized by Prime Minister Ali Abu Ragheb later that month when he visited Baghdad and met with Saddam.

The prime minister's meeting with Saddam was not their first. As minister of trade and industry Abu Ragheb himself negotiated the protocols in 1996 and 1997. In January 1997, the two held meetings en route to the signing of that year's agreement.

The 2001 oil protocol increased the quantity of oil the Kingdom would receive from Iraq from 4.8 million to 5 million tons, an augmentation Jordan had been seeking for a few years to meet (alleged) increased domestic demand. (This equates to Jordan receiving roughly one hundred thousand barrels per day of Iraqi crude.) While the deal reflected a price increase of about $2 from the year 2000 to $20.90 per barrel, the increase was moderate, relatively speaking. Since the previous year's negotiations, the global market price had jumped from $24 to $38 per barrel. Projections of a further increase in price for 2001–2002 also allowed the government to almost double the annual trade protocol to $450 million, a decision widely applauded in the Jordanian industrial and business community.[11]

Although it seemed slight, however, the $2 increase per barrel translated to a $35 million increase in cost deficit to the Jordanian treasury. In line with the specifications of International Monetary Fund (IMF) economic reforms and the stated policy of keeping the deficit under 6 percent of GNP, in 2001 the Kingdom passed these costs onto the consumer by raising the price of gasoline and kerosene.[12] These increases amounted to 15 percent for oil and gas and more than 20 percent in the price of kerosene.[13]

For 2002, the trade protocol was fixed at $206 million, a significant decline from the $309 million in implemented contracts in 2001. Whether this amount would be fully implemented was unclear at the time this study went to press.

It bears mentioning that in addition to signing the protocols, while in Baghdad Abu Ragheb was said to have received a pledge from Iraqi vice president Taha Yassin Ramadan to increase total bilateral trade to $1 billion. This pledge came despite alleged American pressure on Jordan to refrain from further enhancing these ties.[14] In the context of reaching the agreement, Jordan did agree to import from Iraq a sizable amount of sulfur—a chemical mixed with phosphates to manufacture fertilizer, a leading Jordanian industry. Baghdad agreed to provide Jordan with 750,000 tons of this commodity at preferential prices, equating to a cost savings of about 32 percent. Jordan's decision to import sulfur from Iraq was allegedly made in spite of U.S. objections.

In past years, if the Jordanian government set a low trade protocol, the decision was likely based on the speculation that oil prices would be low and therefore the Kingdom's revenue from the sale of that oil would also be low. The logic is as follows: If the protocol is low and the market price of oil increases, Jordan makes a profit. Conversely, if Jordan sets a high trade protocol and the price of oil declines, then Jordan will not be able to generate enough proceeds through sales to cover the cost of the protocol, and the Central Bank of Jordan will be responsible for subsidizing the excess costs.

While setting a lower trade protocol would seem to be the prudent approach, it does have drawbacks. Foremost among these is that the trade protocol essentially equates to a guarantee of Jordanian sales to Iraq. It is likewise widely believed that Jordanian businessmen take advantage of the almost foregone conclusion that the Iraqis will buy to the amount of the protocol, so they do not offer Iraq competitive prices. For these reasons, the Jordanian business community is the leading institutional supporter of increasing the trade protocol as much as possible. (Hence, during negotiations for the 2000 trade protocol, which was eventually set at $300 million, Jordanian industrialists were demanding that the agreement be set at $500 million.) These competing interests engage in an annual policy debate within the Jordanian government, with those championing higher protocols represented by the Ministry of Trade and Industry and those advocating fiscal moderation represented by those in the Central Bank of Jordan.[15]

JORDANIAN EXPORTS TO IRAQ

As with the oil barter arrangement, the Iran–Iraq War ushered in a new era of trade relations between Jordan and Iraq. In the early 1980s, Jordanian industry expanded to serve the market in Iraq, and Jordanian exports to Iraq reached $186 million in 1982. A shortage of resources compelled Iraq to scale back its purchases in 1983, causing Jordanian exports to Iraq to drop to $73 million.[16] To keep trade levels up, Amman provided Baghdad with a line of credit, and subsequently throughout the 1980s, Iraqi purchases of Jordanian products grew steadily. From 1985 to 1989, Jordanian exports to Iraq increased from $168 million to $212.3 million per year.[17] By 1989, the Iraqi market accounted for nearly one-quarter of all Jordanian exports.

Iraq's 1990 invasion of Kuwait reversed, at least temporarily, this upward trend. Jordanian exports to Iraq rebounded to their pre-invasion levels by the mid-1990s, but declined in 1996 following King Hussein's brief support for an initiative to topple Saddam. Table 2.3 shows Jordan's exports from 1989 through 1998.

OIL-FOR-FOOD

Oil protocols amount to grants to the Kingdom of approximately $400–$600 million per year. While these agreements are certainly the most significant aspect of the economic relationship between Jordan and Iraq, the UN-administered Oil-for-Food program has perhaps been the best indicator of the political relationship.

As mentioned earlier, the Oil-for-Food program (also known in Jordan as the Memorandum of Understanding), inaugurated in 1996, is a system whereby Iraq purchases food and medicines by contract and pays for these goods via a UN-controlled bank account in Paris that is funded through oil sales. Unlike the trade protocols (which are limited to Jordan), the Oil-for-Food program provides Baghdad with almost unlimited discretion to determine which countries receive contracts, that is, to decide how to repay its friends. In addition, Oil-for-Food also gives Iraq great flexibility in determining the volume of contracts it can award.[18] The result is that the number of contracts that Jordan receives and the type of products that Iraq purchases

Table 2.3. Jordanian Exports to Iraq in Comparison to Total Jordanian Exports and Gross Total of Exports to All Arab Countries (in millions of JD)

	1989	1991	1995	1996	1997	1998
Gross Jordanian Exports	534.1	598.6	1004.5	1039.8	1067.2	1044.1
Gross Exports to All Arab Countries	241.3	172.3	451.6	485.3	554.2	466.6
Gross Exports to Iraq	123.9	55.8	190.8	96.2	142.1	108.0
Exports to Iraq as a Percentage of Gross Jordanian Exports	23.2%	9.3%	19.0%	9.3%	13.3%	10.3%
Exports to Iraq as a Percentage of Gross Exports to Arab Countries	51.3%	32.4%	42.2%	19.8%	25.6%	23.1%

Source: Amman Chamber of Industry, "Jordanian-Iraqi Economic Relations," June 1999. Based on Statistics from the Central Bank of Jordan.

are, in many ways, more indicative of the state of Jordanian–Iraqi relations than the trade protocols themselves.

A review of the first four years of the Oil-for-Food program shows that Jordan did not receive as large a share of Iraqi contracts as officials expected and businessmen hoped. While Jordan periodically ranks among the highest recipients of Iraqi contracts, the general perception in Jordan is that Iraq has—according to Jordanian businessmen—for some reason penalized Jordan by awarding Jordanian firms a disproportionately smaller share of contracts than they could legitimately have expected to receive. While recent statistics on the Oil-for-Food program are sketchy, there is almost universal sentiment among Jordanian businessmen that this is the case.

In addition, a combination of political and economic factors has contributed to a decline in Jordan's standing as a leading exporter to Iraq. Until the beginning of 1996, Jordan ranked sixth among countries in volume of exports to Iraq. By November 1999, the Kingdom had fallen to number forty-eight.[19] Not surprising given their strong support for Iraq in the UN Security Council, France, Russia, and China have led in Iraqi contract procurement under the Oil-for-Food program as of September 2000 (table 2.4).

What is surprising is Jordan does not even rank as the leading Arab country in terms of contracts. As of September 2000, the value of Iraqi contracts Egypt had secured was almost $300 million more than those Jordan had received. All told, over the course of seven, six-month phases of the program, Jordan had signed contracts with Iraq in excess of $775 million as of August 2000.[20]

Even though Jordan believes it has not received its rightful share of Oil-for-Food contracts, Iraq's influence in the Jordanian economy has grown since the onset of the Oil-for-Food program, with the Jordanian business community increasing pressure on the central government to adopt more Iraq-friendly policies that would be rewarded with more contracts. At the same time, Iraq has expressed displeasure with Jordan by not purchasing certain products in key Jordanian industries or by raising issues of quality with regard to Jordanian products.

Table 2.4. Iraqi Contract Procurement under the Oil-for-Food Program (Humanitarian and Oil Spares), 1996–September 2000

	Number of Contracts	Total Value
France	1,836	$2,607,912,049
Russian Federation	806	$3,142,597,829
China	703	$1,513,746,908
Egypt	456	$1,348,113,054
Australia	32	$1,085,050,000
Jordan	1692	$1,075,116,635
Vietnam	129	$890,311,325

Provided courtesy of the Netherlands Mission to the UN, September 28, 2000.

To a certain extent, Iraqi complaints about Jordanian products have been fair. Prior to the onset of Oil-for-Food, Jordanian industrialists took advantage of the fact that Iraq was a captive market and did not always supply Iraq with quality goods. While delivered products, such as food, sent to Iraq were usually fit for human consumption, they were often older or of lesser quality. One example of this phenomenon was Jordanian juices, which were at times labeled at 250 mls of liquid, but often contained only 220 mls.[21]

After Oil-for-Food was initiated in 1996, the Iraqis began to raise these issues frequently with Jordanian trade officials. With other options available, Baghdad certainly had a legitimate right to speak with its pocketbook and purchase higher-quality goods from other suppliers. At the same time, however, the timing of Baghdad's trade shift away from Amman, shortly after King Hussein declared his support for the Iraqi opposition, was probably not coincidental.

It is difficult to track with specificity the data on exports to Iraq under the Oil-for-Food program (see table 2.5 for the value of Jordanian products exported to Iraq). At one time, detailed information on contracts awarded by country used was posted on the UN Oil-for-Food program website. However,

Table 2.5.   Value of Jordanian Exports to Iraq by Commodity under Oil-for-Food, 1998

Product	Million JD	US Dollars
Table Salt	0.5	704,225.35
Margarine	52.6	74,084,507.04
Hatching Eggs	0.9	1,267,605.63
Local Soaps and Toiletries	24.5	34,507,042.25
Medicine, Antibiotics, Vaccines, Syringes, and Medical Products	24.2	34,084,507.04
Cleaning Detergents	14.9	20,985,915.49
Cheese	1.2	1,690,140.85
Vegetable Oils and Animal Fats	6.3	8,873,239.44
Furniture	4.4	6,197,183.10
Fluid Pumps	1.1	1,549,295.77
Veterinary and Agricultural Pharmaceuticals	3.1	4,366,197.18
Animal Feed Products	0.9	1,267,605.63
Electric Circuits	0.5	704,225.35
Plastic Pipes	0.6	845,070.42
Plastic Bags	0.9	1,267,605.63
Plastics Cases and Polypropylene Backpacks	0.6	845,070.42
Nickel and Curium	0.4	563,380.28
Miscellaneous Including Printing Material, White Cement, Reinforced Steel	0.4	563,380.28

Based on a table provided by the Amman Chamber of Industry, "Jordanian–Iraqi Economic Relations," January 27, 1999.

in 1999 several countries and companies protested this public disclosure, arguing that the posting provided private information detrimental to their competitive advantage in the tender bidding process. The information was taken offline and has not been publicly available since.

Some information on contracts awarded to Jordan is still possible to come by, including the total contract awards per phase. Likewise, the Central Bank of Jordan publishes trade figures on a monthly basis covering the total amount of domestic exports to Iraq. These data are confusing, however, because they do not separate out Jordanian-origin exports from Jordanian reexports (of foreign products). In fact, some Jordanian economists have suggested that the leading beneficiaries of the trade protocols are not Jordanian companies, but rather foreign companies and their Jordanian agents, whose products are reexported via Jordan to Iraq under the terms of the protocol.[22]

Jordan's top two exports to Iraq are covered under Oil-for-Food. They are (1) pharmaceuticals and (2) processed palm oil or "ghee," a product vaguely akin to Crisco.[23] Every day, approximately one hundred Jordanian trucks cross the border bringing foodstuffs and other products contained on the protocol list. Most of these trucks are transiting goods imported via Aqaba rather than indigenous Jordanian exports.

PHARMACEUTICALS

The pharmaceutical industry, with roughly 4,000 employees, was, by 2000, one of Jordan's strongest sectors, and pharmaceuticals were a leading Jordanian export. Iraq is the Kingdom's main export market for this product. While Jordanian pharmaceuticals comprise a specified percentage of the annual trade protocol with Iraq, under the Oil-for-Food program Jordan faces stiff competition from European and other Western drug manufacturers.

In fact, a consistent problem faced by the industry is that despite Iraq's commitment under the trade protocol to the annual purchase of some $50 million in Jordanian drugs, only about $12 million of this total is actually indigenously produced pharmaceuticals.[24] The remainder is reportedly composed of drugs imported to Jordan and reexported via local agents to Baghdad. When the Jordanian Pharmaceutical Manufacturers Association (JPMA) delegations meet with Iraqis, this topic often tops the agenda.

Perhaps the biggest challenge for the pharmaceuticals industry is trying to carve out a larger Jordanian percentage of the Iraqi market. Much of this effort is being made via the Oil-for-Food mechanism. In the competition-free environment prior to the onset of Oil-for-Food, Jordan was quite successful at garnering high market share. Like other industries, however, in a more competitive environment the Kingdom was initially at a disadvantage.

Jordanian pharmaceutical exports to Iraq may have declined, at least in part, due to a problem of quality control. In the early years of the UN sanctions regime, Jordan would ship Iraq older medicines, some of which were close to reaching their expiration dates. Likewise, on occasion and as recently as 1999, medicines of 100 mgs shipped to Iraq only contained 80 mgs of the drug.[25] While it appears that the industry's overall record of quality has improved, Iraqi purchases of these Jordanian products have proven fickle.

In 1998, Jordan was said to have sold some $140 million worth of pharmaceuticals to Iraq. The next year, however, the industry's trade with Iraq bottomed out; some sources reported that sales as of November 1999 had not exceeded $6 million. While noting a sharp decline, more reliable sources reported that in 1999, Iraq imported about 10 percent of its medicines from Jordan, or roughly $27 million.[26] To improve its share, like other industries, the pharmaceuticals sector has been actively attempting to take a higher profile in Baghdad through trade missions and meetings with top-level Iraqi officials. Toward this goal, JPMA has done quite well. In 1999, a JPMA delegation to Baghdad held well-publicized discussions with Iraqi vice president Taha Yassin Ramadan. In September of that year, reports indicated that Iraqi authorities (with the agreement of the UN Sanctions Committee) had decided "to earmark most of the funds allotted for the importation of medicines within the Oil-for-Food program for importing Jordanian medicines."[27] The Iraqis also committed to purchasing another $20 million worth of Jordanian medicines. While official Iraqi purchase pledges are often not reliable, it appears that this commitment was bona fide.

During a visit to Amman in November, following up on the September decision, the Iraqi minister of health held meetings with his Jordanian counterparts as well as officials from the JPMA. After these discussions, the minister announced Baghdad's intention to increase Iraq's annual purchases from $20 million to $32 million.[28] In February 2000, Iraq's trade minister confirmed that Iraq had indeed increased its purchases of medical products from Jordan. He also took the opportunity to note that the Kingdom's pharmaceutical companies were the leading exporters to Iraq under the Oil-for-Food program.[29] Figures issued by the Jordanian Department of Statistics in December 2000 confirmed a 30 percent increase in the Kingdom's drug exports to Baghdad that year, and forecast—based on an Iraqi decision to allow the private sector to import pharmaceuticals—that the exports from this sector to Iraq would increase from 10 to 15 percent in 2001.[30] The predictions, by and large, appear to have been accurate; in 2001, Jordanian pharmaceutical exports to Iraq totaled 25 million Euros, approximately $25 million.[31]

It is too early to tell what (if any) the long-term effect of Jordan's implementation of intellectual property (IP) regulations in the Kingdom will have on sales to the Iraqi market. While IP helped Jordan gain entry into the World

Trade Organization (WTO) and obtain a Free Trade Agreement (FTA) with the United States, these regulations have started to cripple the pharmaceuticals industry, which has traditionally relied on production of nonlicensed (i.e., pirated) Western-produced drugs.

Currently, the Iraqi market does not have a high demand for many of these products; however, if and when the sanctions eventually end and Iraq once again becomes a prosperous economy, the Baghdad middle class may start to clamor for cutting-edge drugs that are not yet available in the less exclusive (licensed) generic format. If and when this time comes, such a development may prove the death knell for Jordan's pharmaceuticals industry.

PRIVATE TRADE

In addition to the trade protocol system and the Oil-for-Food mechanism, there is a small but thriving cash and barter trade between the two states that occurs outside the framework of UN monitoring. This shadowy world often involves cash transactions done with the acquiescence of Jordanian authorities and the approval of Baghdad. No reliable public statistics are available regarding this trade, which is, according to international standards, illegal. Hence, the extent of the phenomenon is impossible to ascertain.

While officials are not quick to publicize the cash and barter trade, there appears to be some tacit promotion of it. In February 1999, Hamud al-Qatarneh, the Jordanian ambassador to Iraq, noted that private trade offered an excellent opportunity for the Jordanian businessman. He stated: "It's no secret that a lot of Arab and foreign states are dealing with the Iraqi market via barter arrangements. This practice is widespread in Baghdad and it's possible to do outside of any [UN] agreements."[32] How this nonauthorized trade is accomplished is not exactly clear. As one Jordanian businessman with close ties to Baghdad confided, however, the first question Iraqis typically ask is, "Will you take oil?" Still, this businessman added that not too many Jordanians participate in the barter trade, because the logistics are difficult. With Jordanian refineries already operating at capacity, the oil would have to be processed elsewhere.

SMUGGLING

As both Jordan and Iraq are tribally based societies with borders that were, until recently, mostly unguarded and often undemarcated, smuggling is—not surprisingly—a common occurrence along the Jordan–Iraq frontier. While the onset of UN sanctions against Iraq in August 1990—and the subsequent imposition of trade supervision by the London-based insurance firm Lloyd's Register—limited this practice, it did not end it. Smuggling between Jordan and Iraq primarily entails the cross-border transfer of goods without the knowledge of the two states' governments. In some cases, however, there have also been transfers of goods between the states with official acquiescence. For purposes of definition, this latter trade—which skirts UN monitoring—is also considered smuggling.

Throughout the 1990s, the level and quality of this trade varied. In the early part of the decade, for example, there were allegations that both the Iraqi and Jordanian governments permitted luxury consumer items (not allowed under UN regulations), such as whiskey, cigarettes, and automobiles, to travel from Jordan to Iraq. Likewise, reports indicated that Russian military spare parts made their way into Iraq overland from Jordan. There is some indication that the UN sanctions inspection regime in Aqaba did prevent some Iraqi-bound contraband from entering Jordan.

Still, the ongoing legal traffic of oil and products across the Jordan–Iraq border—as well as the longtime Iraqi involvement in the Kingdom's economic and banking systems—appears to have contributed to an environment conducive to illicit trade. As a result, foreign diplomats typically complained of Jordan's lax enforcement of the sanctions during those years even as the Kingdom attempted to maintain the veneer of compliance.

In addition to this illegal trade carried out with the knowledge of both Amman and Baghdad, there appears to have been, at least until 1995, a thriving practice of traditional "smuggling"—done without the knowledge of either government. While the numbers on smuggling are difficult to ascertain, the border between Jordan and Iraq, which resembles the international border between Arizona and Mexico, is well suited for it. Furthermore, while the Kingdom has no doubt made great efforts to prevent the flow of contraband—particularly weapons—from entering Jordan, it is less clear how much effort the Jordanians have made to prevent their own consumer goods from flowing into Iraq outside the supervision of the UN.

To some degree, the extent of smuggling over the past decade appears to be related to the state of political relations between Amman and Baghdad. In August 1995—following the arrival of Iraqi asylum-seeker Hussein Kamel and King Hussein's subsequent address calling for the removal of Saddam—the political relationship between Jordan and Iraq underwent a transformation, as did the Kingdom's policy vis-à-vis sanctions enforcement and border security. Following these incidents, it was reported that Jordanian forces tightened security measures on the border, resulting in delays of up to ten hours for those traveling from Amman to Baghdad.

In late August 1995, Jordanian forces apprehended five Iraqis on route to Amman. Authorities maintain that the Iraqis, who were carrying automatic weapons, were planning attacks in the Jordanian capital. One week later, Jordanian forces captured an alleged Iraqi suicide bomber en route to Amman. Following these episodes, the Kingdom appears to have initiated a concerted effort to improve its border security, which included doubling the height (to almost twelve feet) of a sand wall spanning the 108-mile border with Iraq and increasing the number of checkpoints along the Baghdad–Amman highway. (A ten-foot-deep trench running the length of the border had already been built in 1993–1994.)[33]

In contrast to the previous four years, Jordanian authorities stopped a number of illegal shipments in the months that followed the Kamel defection. Of particular note were the November 1995 seizure of Russian-made gyroscopes (for use in Iraqi missiles) and the December 1995 confiscation of "dangerous substances," both en route to Iraq. This trend continued into 1996, when in March Jordanian customs officials stopped a shipment of military material bound for Baghdad. Despite these seizures, smuggling continued to be a problem—particularly Iraqi contraband (i.e., weapons) entering the Kingdom, which threatened Jordanian stability.

So serious was this issue that in January 1997 King Hussein made a trip to inspect Jordan's eastern border. During his visit, he noted with concern that the Iraqi and Jordanian smugglers were utilizing the latest technology—satellite communications and modern weaponry.[34] He likewise confirmed that the illicit trade of goods constituted only a secondary concern. "Sheep are not the only problem," the king said, "there are drugs . . . in addition to weapons and explosives."

In his speech to the Desert Forces and Border Guards, King Hussein promised his troops better equipment, including night-vision glasses, to increase the efficacy of their operations. The Kingdom received some of this equipment from the United States in 1997. Even so, as then minister of the interior Nathir Rashid later pointed out, "Jordan's resources are modest compared with those at the disposal of these gangs" of smugglers.[35] To further hamper this illegal activity, the Kingdom augmented its security presence on the border with regular army units and some mechanized units. Effectively, the king split the Bedouin forces—which were then responsible for border security—into two parts. One part was dedicated to public security, while the other half was released to the armed forces and retrained for border control detail.

Still, indications suggest that these changes did little to limit or end the illicit activity. In fact, throughout late 1998 and early 1999 Jordanian border guards engaged in almost nightly battles—involving mortars and antitank missiles—with well-armed Iraqi smugglers in the border area. While some would suggest that Iraqi soldiers provide assistance to the smugglers for money, this participation is thought to be out of Baghdad's control.

Indeed, the situation for Iraqi troops stationed on the border is said to be quite pitiful. One Jordanian minister whispered that it was commonplace for Iraqi soldiers to sell their guns to Jordanian soldiers.[36] These guns were preferable, he said, because they were "untraceable." Likewise, it is said that Jordanian troops serving in the border area often fed their Iraqi counterparts, who had no food or money.

By the time King Abdullah acceded to the throne in February 1999, bilateral relations had significantly improved from 1995, but the border situation remained tense. In April 2000, for example, the Jordanian state security court sentenced three Iraqi smugglers to ten years in prison for illegal weapons trafficking to Jordan. These men, part of a larger ring, were caught bringing in 130 Kalashnikovs and 17 machine guns in 1999.

The Jordanian and Iraqi ministers of interior met in Amman in October 1999 to discuss issues of border security. At the time, the two were reported to have signed an agreement to fight drug and weapons trafficking between the two states. In return for this cooperation, the Kingdom was said to have agreed to repatriate Iraqi citizens—particularly conscripted deserters—illegally crossing the border.

More recently, in light of warming bilateral relations, Jordanian officials have been playing down the weapons trade and implicit Iraqi attempts to destabilize the Kingdom. In October 1999, Jordan's minister of labor suggested that, unlike the early 1990s, smuggling only involved "animals, skins, and drugs."[37] According to the minister of transportation, most of the illegal commodities crossing the border consisted of electronics, food, sulfur, uria, dates, wool, and oil.[38] Even so, the United States that year allotted $8 million in "nonmilitary aid," funding typically allocated for border control equipment expenditures.

Despite improved border protection measures in the King Abdullah era, smuggling clearly remains a problem for Jordan. After September 11, 2001, Jordanian officials reported dramatic increases in infiltration attempts. Many of the apprehended were attempting to bring weapons from Syria and Iraq to assist the Palestinians in the armed intifada against Israel.[39]

TRANSPORT INDUSTRY AND SANCTIONS ENFORCEMENT

Jordan's port of Aqaba and the Kingdom's impressive transport industry were developed in the 1980s during the heyday of Jordanian–Iraqi trade. During the years of the Iran–Iraq War, when Jordan served as the primary transit route for Iraq-bound goods, Aqaba was expanded and Jordan's trucking fleet blossomed into one of the most modern and well equipped in the Middle East. The Aqaba-to-Baghdad highway was so well traveled by Jordanian truckers that, over time, it made economic sense to replace the asphalt pavement with more durable (but exponentially more expensive) concrete.

The Jordanian role as entrepôt to Iraq was not based on economic rationale. Rather, it was born out of wartime necessity. Over time, however, the Kingdom's economy adjusted and benefited greatly from the transit service provided to its eastern neighbor. In the years before Iraq's invasion of Kuwait, Aqaba handled some 20 million tons of goods per year, about 7 million of which were destined for Iraq. The land transit industry that moved this cargo supported some 250,000 people in Jordan (via 12,000 trucks), as well as those en route serving this sector.[40] Even at the currently depressed levels—which as of early 2000 equated to roughly 12 million tons arriving via Aqaba mostly for domestic consumption—the transport sector in Jordan contributes 13 percent of Jordan's gross domestic product.[41]

Although it can handle one-hundred-thousand-ton ships and is considered a centerpiece of the Kingdom's plans for economic development, in recent decades Aqaba has not been known for its efficiency or its reasonable prices. Likewise, the Jordanian port was, for most of the 1990s, saddled with Lloyd's Register, which handled the UN-mandated inspections of all Iraq-bound goods entering Aqaba.

AQABA UTILIZATION AND UN MONITORING

The Jordanian role in sanctions enforcement was not one that the Kingdom willingly accepted or relished. Indeed, in August 1990 after the UN Security Council (UNSC) passed Resolution 661—the resolution authorizing economic sanctions against Iraq—Amman continued trading with Baghdad for several weeks. Only after the U.S. Navy instituted a blockade of Aqaba did Jordan start to comply with some of the measures stipulated in the UNSC resolution. In October 1990, the U.S. Department of State eventually certified Jordan's compliance with sanctions. Still, leakage to Iraq via Jordan remained a significant concern for the UN Sanctions Committee.

Less than one month after the passage of UNSC 661, Amman petitioned the Sanctions Committee for relief under Article 50 of the UN Charter, which allows that any state "which finds itself confronted with special economic problems arising from the carrying out of those [UNSC enforcement] measures shall have the right to consult the Security Council with regard to a solution of those problems." Under this provision, Jordan proposed that the committee formally allow the Kingdom to continue importing oil from Iraq. While recognizing the unique nature of the Kingdom's economic hardship, the committee nonetheless made an internal determination that the continuation of Jordanian oil imports would constitute a violation of UN sanctions.

(Indeed, when India petitioned the committee for similar dispensation in January 1991, it was summarily rejected.)[42] Nevertheless, no action was taken against Jordan for ongoing imports of Iraqi oil, which were interrupted only briefly during Operation Desert Storm.

In May 1991, after the expulsion of Iraq from Kuwait, Jordan sent a letter informing the committee that it had resumed importation of Iraqi oil. According to Paul Conlon, a German committee member from 1990 to 1995, the committee "took note" of this development but took no action against it. Essentially, the committee decided to "tolerate and legalize" Jordan's imports from Iraq.[43] Over the course of the next few years, Jordan periodically reported to the committee on how much oil it was importing.

While Amman received a pass from the UN on its oil imports, it had no such luck with its exports and reexports (via Aqaba) to Iraq. From 1990 through 1994, per UNSC resolutions, all shipments entering Jordan via the port of Aqaba were subject to at-sea inspection by the Maritime Interception Force (MIF). Jordanian shipping agents complained bitterly about the expense and problems imposed by MIF inspections. Primarily, the complaints were related to the fact that all containers on ships bound for Aqaba had to be accessible to inspectors boarding the ships.

Given the way that containers are closely stacked for sea voyages, the MIF mission created a host of logistical problems—including lengthy delays and added expenses—for Jordanian shipping agents. In order to comply with the strict inspection regulations, which specified that containers be stacked only three high, ships often had to limit their available cargo capacities by up to 30 percent. As such, the inspection surcharge for a standard forty-foot container could reach one thousand dollars.[44] As a result of the additional costs, nearly half of the forty-one shipping lines that had previously serviced Aqaba stopped calling on the Jordanian port.

But to Jordanians the MIF inspections were more than just an economic problem; they constituted an unfair violation of Jordanian sovereignty. Jordanians complained that the Kingdom was being singled out for monitoring while, as one Jordanian minister charged, "Turkey is violating [and] Syria is openly violating [by] sending goods to Iraq."[45] More than one commentator described the inspections as "an affront to Jordan which the Jordanian people cannot tolerate."[46]

In April 1994, Jordanian and U.S. officials finally agreed to employ Lloyd's Register to carry out shore-based inspections. The cost to Jordan to retain Lloyd's Register was $3 million per year. This was far less expensive and more politically acceptable than the previous arrangement, which, according to some Jordanian sources, cost Amman $1.3 billion in freight and other charges.[47]

The success of the MIF program in preventing entry of prohibited materials into Iraq is difficult to ascertain. In four years, the MIF carried out over twenty thousand inspections and failed to seize any illegal goods.[48] Clearly, however, the seaborne searches had a deleterious effect on Aqaba. From 1989 through 1994, transit imports via Aqaba to Iraq decreased by 79 percent in terms of tonnage.[49]

While Jordanian shippers and businessmen were initially pleased with the changeover from MIF enforcement to Lloyd's Register, they quickly became disenchanted with the new regime. One former minister of trade and industry commented that the Lloyd's arrangement was "turning out to be a cumbersome and time-consuming procedure."[50]

In 1996, like other Jordanian industries, the port was hit hard by the onset of the UN Oil-for-Food program. Given a choice—and with Aqaba still under the close supervision of Lloyd's—Iraq chose to diversify its port utilization. Instead of Aqaba, Iraq starting shipping its UN-approved commodities through Syria and the United Arab Emirates. In subsequent years, in an effort to be more competitive and induce a return of Iraq-bound products to Aqaba, it is rumored that Amman lobbied Egypt to reduce the tariff rates on Iraq-bound goods transiting via Suez to Jordan. (Table 2.6 shows statistics on Port of Aqaba usage from 1990 to 1999.)[51] While Iraqi usage of Aqaba picked up the following year, Jordanian complaints about the limited level of Iraqi transit shipments through Aqaba persisted through the death of King Hussein.

In October 1999, Jordanian minister of trade and industry Muhammed Asfour traveled to Baghdad to attend the International Trade Fair (where Jordanian companies filled one hundred booths) and to hold meetings with his Iraqi counterparts. A primary objective on Asfour's agenda was to increase

Table 2.6.   Statistics on Port of Aqaba Transit Usage, 1990–1999

Year	Tons
1990	3,154,394
1991	1,439,541
1992	1,959,465
1993	1,036,097
1994	193,841
1995	512,599
1996	278,002
1997	592,556
1998	510,018
1999	411,011

Iraqi utilization of the Aqaba port. Six months earlier, Iraqi officials had agreed to import 70 percent of their total imports through Aqaba, but this pledge, like many others, had yet to materialize.

Prior to his Baghdad visit, to entice the Iraqis to return to Aqaba, Asfour had implemented tariff reductions on Iraq-bound commodities to make the Kingdom's port more competitive with Tartus in Syria.[52] This move was designed to counter the Iraqi charge that cost was the principal reason why Aqaba had fallen into disfavor in Baghdad.

While in Baghdad, Asfour lobbied the Iraqis—including Vice President Taha Yassin Ramadan and Deputy Prime Minister Tariq Aziz—to "invigorate" the port of Aqaba. Appealing to primarily noneconomic rationale, Asfour reportedly told them: "The Jordanian-Iraqi relations could not be linked to or assessed on the basis of shipping charges here or there. This is because the relationship between the two sides is stronger than materialistic influences."[53] Aqaba was essential, Asfour argued, because it would invigorate other Jordanian economic sectors like land transport.

After the meetings, Asfour publicly praised "the spirit of cooperation that prevailed" in his Baghdad get-togethers.[54] Later, however, he noted that the discussions were quite tense. During one of his meetings with Ramadan and Iraqi minister of trade Muhammad Mahdi Saleh, Asfour stated that it was in the hands of Iraq to prevent Aqaba from becoming "a ghost city." In the strongest of terms, Asfour then pleaded: "It shouldn't be done!"[55] Saleh and Ramadan were, apparently, offended by Asfour's tone. (One month later, Asfour was sacked.)

Press reports after the trade mission returned indicated some preliminary success, including an agreement in principle that Iraq would ship 157,000 tons of wheat via Aqaba. Asfour was also promised separately that the total would be increased to 300,000 tons of Iraq-bound wheat transited via Aqaba,[56] a pledge amounting to roughly half of Iraq's total annual wheat imports. In addition, it was reported that the two countries agreed to boost overland transport of goods by the jointly owned Iraqi–Jordanian Land Transport Company. However, in spite of the optimistic reports, while some wheat shipments bound for Iraq did eventually arrive, overall there was little follow-through on the Aqaba agreements reached in November 1999.

Aqaba made headlines once again in May 2000 when reports surfaced that the government was considering deep reductions on shipment fees for Iraq-bound goods.[57] These reports were confirmed when, on July 11, the Jordanian cabinet approved unprecedented across-the-board cuts on most portage fees. Among other decreases, the tariff reductions included a 50 percent decrease on containerized and general (nonrefrigerated) cargos as well as a 50 percent cut on the use of suction machines for grain discharge (from 1.400 Jordanian dinars [JD] to .700 JD per ton). In addition, the government reduced land transportation charges by about 25 percent from 22.500 JD to 17.600 JD per ton.[58]

Preliminary signs that these initiatives would get results came that August (not coincidentally) at about the same time King Abdullah was brokering a political rapprochement with Iraq. Early that month, Iraqi officials announced that during renovations on Basra airport, Baghdad would increase its utilization of Aqaba for imports and for exporting from the region.[59] In September, shortly after King Abdullah spoke of bilateral relations turning a "new page," the Jordanian minister of transport announced that Iraq was ready to commence increased utilization of Aqaba. He noted that two ships brimming with rice and wheat intended for Iraq were en route to Aqaba.[60]

Interestingly, one week after the minster's announcement, the Jordanian government submitted a formal request to the UN to end the Lloyd's Register inspections.[61] Then, in October, Jordan unilaterally expelled Lloyd's. Although it is too early to tell, indications suggest that, as many would have predicted, the departure of Lloyd's has "encouraged" Iraq to return to importing via the port of Aqaba."[62]

If the removal of Lloyd's does not encourage Baghdad to revive trade through Jordan's port, the drop in Jordanian prices on July 16, 2000, may. This price decrease made Aqaba much more competitive vis-à-vis its archrival port, Jebal Ali in Dubai. A comparison of prices for twenty-foot containers—the industry standard—tells the story. With the discount, shipment of a container via Aqaba costs about 30 JD, or about $45. The comparable shipment via Jebal Ali cost about $70.[63]

Another area of economic cooperation and contention has been the Iraqi–Jordanian Land Transport Company, a governmental company established in 1980 to serve as the means for transporting products during the Iran–Iraq War from the port of Aqaba to Iraq and later to play a central role in the shipment of Iraqi oil to Jordan.[64] Iraqi utilization of this company has varied dramatically over the years, peaking in 1987 at over 1.4 million tons per year. In 2000, annual shipments amounted to less than one-tenth of that amount. In 1996 when bilateral relations between Iraq and Jordan were at their darkest hour, so too was the utilization of this company. (Table 2.7 shows the company's annual shipments in tons from 1981 through 2000.)

With the decline in tonnage and an increase in gasoline prices, profits for the company have fallen as well, from more than $2 million in the mid-1980s to just $385,000 in 1997.[65] In part, the declining tonnage is indicative of the stiffer competition in Jordan for shipping work. Also, it appears that Saddam's preference to "spread the wealth"—particularly to Egypt, which has been providing Iraq with considerable political support toward ending sanctions—has resulted in an increase in business for the joint Iraqi, Egyptian, and Jordanian shipping company known as the "Arab Bridge." Indeed, in January 2001,

Table 2.7.   Iraqi–Jordanian Land Transport Company Annual Shipments in Tons, 1981–2000

Year	Products Transported from Jordan to Iraq (in Tons)	Oil Transported from Iraq to Jordan (in Tons)	Total Tons Per Year
1981	6,293	0	6,293
1982	745,021	0	745,021
1983	896,115	0	896,115
1984	974,489	0	974,489
1985	1,084,418	0	1,084,418
1986	1,201,352	0	1,201,352
1987	1,422,818	0	1,422,818
1988	1,295,897	0	1,295,897
1989	1,289,855	0	1,289,855
1990	808,668	0	808,668
1991	370,160	0	370,160
1992	307,357	0	307,357
1993	372,420	0	372,420
1994	157,118	97,797	254,915
1995	117,694	17,209	134,903
1996	80,292	22,481	102,773
1997	114,697	103,939	218,636
1998	97,279	137,536	234,815
1999	57,390	127,555	184,945
2000	45,953	85,197	131,150

Statistics provided by the Iraqi–Jordanian Land Transport Company.

Egyptian president Hosni Mubarak hosted Iraqi vice president Ramadan for the first high-level Egyptian–Iraqi bilateral meetings in ten years. The meetings culminated with the signing of a Free Trade Agreement between the two countries. Following the visit, Ramadan reported that Cairo and Baghdad were in the process of considering an upgrade of their diplomatic representation to the ambassadorial level.[66]

During a visit to Baghdad in October 1999, Asfour, still Jordanian minister of trade and industry, tried to convince Iraq to direct more business toward the Iraqi–Jordanian joint company. Iraqi officials, however, indicated a predilection toward the Arab Bridge.

ALTERNATIVES TO IRAQ: LIMITED OPTIONS?

"Everyone likes to deal with Iraq."[67] This sentiment, articulated by First Secretary of the Amman Chamber of Commerce Yanal al Bustami, is echoed almost uniformly within the Kingdom's business community. For Jordanians, the rationale is simple: dealing with Iraq is perceived to be relatively easy and extremely profitable.

Munir Soubir, the head of the Economic Committee of the lower house of Jordan's parliament, attributes the Jordanian preference for Iraq to three factors: first, Iraqis need everything; second, Jordanians have strong humanitarian concerns for Iraqis; and third, dealings with the UN (and by extension Iraq) are "100 percent insured."[68] Likewise, as shipping magnate Tawfiq Kawar points out, because of government procurement, "Iraqis can afford to buy quality [i.e., expensive] products."[69] In this sense, he says, the "Iraqi consumer" is better than other regional alternatives.

But the Jordanian attraction to the Iraqi market is not solely a result of the profit motive. To some extent, historic ties dating back to the days when the Hashemites ruled both Amman and Baghdad play a minor but still important role in the close bilateral economic ties. More significant is the fact that many top-ranking officials in the Jordanian government bureaucracy today were educated in Baghdad in the 1960s, including the top echelon of economic decision makers, for example, the governor and deputy governor of the Central Bank of Jordan. (For more on this theme, see chapter 4.)

Perhaps more than the positive feelings in Amman, however, the Jordanian inclination toward Iraq is stimulated by Jordan's ambivalent sentiments toward its other neighbors and potential trade partners, particularly Syria and Israel. Geographically, trade with Israel and Syria would make more sense for Jordan than transporting goods eight hundred kilometers across harsh desert terrain to Iraq. The costs associated with transport alone place many of Jordan's exports (such as cement) beyond a shipping radius that makes economic sense. Even so, the Kingdom's businessmen have not capitalized on their western or northern neighbors as lucrative trade partners. The reasons for these underdeveloped ties vary for Syria and Israel, respectively.

A series of stereotypes and procedural difficulties contribute to what amounts to a Jordanian aversion to dealing with the Syrian business community. Although it is larger than the Kingdom, Syria is seen as a small market producing many products similar to those made in Jordan. Perhaps more harmful to potential trade, though, are the prevailing perceptions of Syrians in Jordan. Iraqis—as individuals and as a government—are believed by Jordanians to be the "most magnanimous" of all the Kingdom's trading partners. Whereas Jordanians perceive Iraqis as "straight shooters"—one Jordanian described them as the "most honest in the Arab world"—they fear business dealings with Damascene businessmen, who they say are among the most cunning and duplicitous in the region. According to one former Jordanian politician of Palestinian origin, "Iraqis are not shrewd traders, they are bedu [i.e., Bedouin]. Syrian merchants are shrewd bastards."

In addition to these prevalent Jordanian stereotypes of Syrians, several procedural barriers discourage a stronger north–south trade. There is simply much less "red tape" for Jordanians exporting to Iraq or Saudi Arabia than to Syria. If a Jordanian businessman wants to export to Syria, for example, he needs an order from the Syrian Ministry of Trade, a letter from the Central Bank of Syria proving that there is enough foreign currency to cover the transaction, and a completed price survey from the Ministry of Trade to ensure the competitiveness of the product.[70] Even after all these procedures, proper payment is not ensured. Contrary to signed agreements, the Syrian Central Bank sometimes makes payments in the nonliquid Syrian lira or sometimes even in barter payment.[71] Business with Iraq is simpler and swifter. There, the government is the only buyer. After Baghdad authorizes an Iraqi bank to make a purchase, a letter is issued, and the deal is finished.

With Israel, Jordanian merchants encounter a different set of problems. These relate mostly to protectionism and security procedures that combine to frustrate Jordanian trade with the West Bank, a $2 billion market that was once critical to Jordan's economy. In 1999, former Jordanian deputy prime minister Rima Khalaf blamed Israeli "protectionism under a security pretext, and the desire to keep control of a captive Palestinian market" for the low levels of Jordanian trade in these Israeli-controlled areas.[72] To be sure, security has proven a leading concern for the Israelis, and this priority has been reflected in the cumbersome bureaucratic procedures inflicted on Jordanian exporters. Not only do Jordanian goods entering the Palestinian Authority (PA) require export licensure from Israel, but they also are subjected to a tedious inspection regimen. Through the end of 2000, for example, with the exception of cement, all Jordanian trucks carrying goods across the border had to be off-loaded onto an Israeli truck via the "back-to-back" procedure, at a prohibitive cost to the (Palestinian) consumer of five dollars per crate.[73] These cumbersome procedures have since been modified, but significant procedural and protectionist barriers still exist, undermining transport and trade between Jordan and the PA.

Stringent Israeli import regulations to the PA have not encouraged Jordanian exporters. Ironically, as Jordanian exports to Palestinians have remained flat, in recent years Jordanian exports to Israel itself have increased. In 2000, for example, Jordanian exports to Israel increased by over 25 percent, and this trade continues to increase. A comparison of January–June statistics from 2001 and 2002 shows an increase from $19 million to $24 million.[74]

This increase in trade with Israel is noteworthy, particularly given the Palestinian intifada and the virulent "anti-normalization" campaign that is so powerful in Jordan. The campaign, orchestrated by a consortium of Islamist and radical pan-Arabist groups and parties, takes several shapes. Typically, the anti-normalizers—led by the Council of Professional Associations or the

Anti-Normalization Committee—publish a "blacklist" in an Islamist newspaper (such as *al-Sabil*) of those people and companies doing business with Israel. In February 2001, for example, the committee published a list of sixty-eight names, including thirty-two companies, two private schools, a hotel, a newspaper, and some high-ranking Jordanian officials.[75] As with other lists, the expressed request was for the readership to boycott these companies. More than just an economic penalty, though, there is, with the publication of this type of list, an implicit physical threat.

Then, of course, there is the issue of the secondary boycott instituted by Iraq. Many of the industrialists in Jordan who would be most eligible for selling their wares in Tel Aviv are currently doing a substantial amount of business with Baghdad. The risk associated with entering the Israeli market is clear and present. Indeed, the stated policy of Iraq is not to do business with companies that deal with Israel. In 1999, the Jordanian daily *al-Dustur* ran a story about one Jordanian pharmaceutical company that had dealings with Israel. Almost immediately, Iraqi officials effectively blacklisted the company from the Iraqi market.[76] As one Jordanian businessman put it, "We're afraid to deal with 'our cousins' [the Jews] because of our dealings with Iraq." In a more colorful analogy, another industrialist who has a lot of dealings with Iraq compared working with the Israelis to having an extra-marital affair: "Everyone wants to," he said, "but you're afraid that your wife [i.e., Iraq] will find out."

Given the difficulties with Israel and Syria, it is almost natural that Jordan would gravitate toward Iraq. As a senior Jordanian official once said to Secretary of State Madeleine Albright, "Jordan is closed on the North, South and East. What should Jordan do, close Iraq?" To abandon Iraq as Jordan's leading trading partner would, according to former foreign minister Marwan al-Qassem, "leave me orphaned here and orphaned there."[77]

THE ECONOMIC ORIENTATION OF JORDAN

There is an ongoing debate in Jordan regarding the disposition of the Kingdom's economic future. The division between the popularly elected lower house of parliament and the king's appointed upper house reflects polarization on this question. In capsule form, the debate is as follows: many of Jordan's elites are receptive to enhanced economic relations with Israel, an economic powerhouse and gateway to the Mediterranean and the West, while most of Jordan's populace prefer to place the nation's economic bet on closer ties with Iraq, hoping for an eventual return to the heyday of the 1980s.

Since his ascension to the throne, King Abdullah has tried to have it both ways, seeking expanded trade eastward and westward. In addition, he has undertaken a concerted effort to repair ties with Persian Gulf countries and to strengthen traditionally close ties with the United States. Indeed, King Abdullah seems to have opted for a policy of "friend to all" when it comes to seeking allies to help Jordan's ailing economy. So far, the king's efforts have included privatizing of major government industries, streamlining bureaucratic procedures, and concerted fighting against governmental corruption. Most significantly, the Kingdom has embarked on a program of legislative reform geared toward establishing an environment more conducive to foreign investment and more amenable to doing business with Europe and the United States. In particular, the king has made great efforts to convince Western investors that Jordan's high-technology labor force could transform the Kingdom into an Arab "silicon valley." Together, these initiatives eased Jordan's February 2000 entry into the WTO. In part, they also encouraged the United States to sign an FTA with Jordan in November 2000. Finally ratified in September 2001, Jordan became the only Arab state both to be a member of the WTO and to have an FTA with the United States. Given these developments, most Jordanian businessmen are cautiously optimistic about the future.

Still, the attraction toward Iraq remains strong. Given the proven economic benefits of the bilateral relationship, there is a prevalent sense in the Kingdom's business community that there is and always will be an organic economic link between Iraq and Jordan. As one businessman expressed it, there is a "connected destiny" for the two economies.[78] This understanding underlies the belief that in its future trade relations with Jordan, Baghdad's decision making will not be based primarily on economic rationale.

As Mrawid al-Tel, a former adviser to King Hussein, explains it, Iraq's future behavior vis-à-vis Jordan will be formed by its Arab nationalism. Iraqis, he says, are "sincere about pan-Arabism. . . . this is why Saddam helps Jordan."[79] Interestingly, many Jordanians believe that this Arab nationalism—and an Iraqi sense of gratitude for Jordan's loyalty—will sway Baghdad toward a more favorable economic disposition vis-à-vis the Kingdom. Zarqa's chamber of industry head Muhammed al-Tel expresses this point of view in stating that "Iraq understands the Jordanian economic situation which carried a tremendous burden during the Gulf War."[80] The burden, he notes, came about as a result of Jordan's "support for our dear Iraqi brothers."

The Jordanian belief that Saddam is a true Arab nationalist who will remember and eventually repay the Kingdom is not limited to the business community; it is common among some top Jordanian government officials as well. Jordanian minister of labor Eid al-Fayez, for example, holds that "Iraq rewards those who stand with them." Hence, it logically follows that "when sanctions are over, Jordan will be the number one country to benefit."[81] The one possible thorn in this scenario, as even Iraqi sympathizers note, is the possibility that in the post-sanctions era Saddam will decide to punish Jordan for acceding to the sanctions, or a post-Saddam Iraq will punish Jordan for maintaining such an intimate relationship with Saddam. As of 2001, however, higher protocols, more trade links, and increased Iraqi utilization of Aqaba suggested an overall progression toward closer bilateral economic relations.

Ironically, even the increased U.S. financial support for Jordan under King Abdullah may contribute to Jordan's closer economic cooperation with Baghdad. After all, given Jordan's new sources of support, Saddam may feel compelled to compete or risk a less dependent (and potentially less pliant) Jordan. In the end, the extent of Jordan's economic dependence on Baghdad only heightens Iraq's ability to manipulate policy in Amman. In this regard, the strongly held belief in Jordan that in the post-sanctions era Jordan is likely to "do more business with Iraq than the 1980s" is itself reason for concern.[82]

TRADE AS A TOOL OF IRAQI MANIPULATION

After 1996, when the UN's Oil-for-Food program opened Iraqi commerce to global competition, the Kingdom's near monopoly on trade with Baghdad disappeared. Since then, as the "playing field" has expanded, Jordan has found it increasingly difficult to maintain its share of the Iraqi market. Still, in spite of its competitive disadvantage and the sometimes severe fluctuations in bilateral trade between the states, Jordan has found a way to remain a significant player in the Iraqi market.

Jordan's perseverance with Iraq is driven by economic necessity; quite simply, Jordan has few alternatives. Likewise, at least in part, Jordan's staying power in Iraq is attributable to bilateral historical ties as well as the strong personal relations and goodwill that have developed over time. In terms of decision making, it would appear that for the Kingdom, the economic imperative outweighs all potentially negative consequences of the relationship. Like Jordan, Iraq derives several benefits from the bilateral economic ties. The difference is that for Iraq these benefits have been primarily political.

Since 1996, Saddam has pursued an economic policy of carrots and sticks geared toward ending Iraq's international isolation. A CIA report leaked in September 2000 discussed the interplay between economics and sanctions busting and suggested that Iraq is giving UN Oil-for-Food contracts to states proffering "antisanctions rhetoric."[83] Iraq's policy toward Germany and Japan exemplifies Saddam's strategy. Prior to the Gulf War, these states were some of Iraq's leading suppliers. By fall 2000, they accounted for but 1 percent of total contracts. In that same period, France, Russia, and China—among the most vocal advocates for ending the sanctions—accounted for one-third of

these deals. The Iraqi strategy appears to have paid off; by awarding contracts, Saddam purchased international support for loosening UNSC constraints.

Although well below the level of France and Russia, Jordan, too, has
played a significant role in this Iraqi policy. In fact, during the first two years
of King Abdullah's reign, contrary to the King Hussein era, the Kingdom has
proven the most ardent Middle Eastern state advocating an end to UN sanctions. And during this period, the Kingdom's Iraq policy has seemed to be
uncharacteristically appreciated by Baghdad. Highlights from 2000 include
a sanctions-busting flight from Amman to Baghdad and visits to Iraq by the
prime minister and foreign minister of Jordan. These high-profile firsts set
the stage for Iraq's regional reintegration. The year 2000 also saw the removal by King Abdullah of Abdel Karim al-Kabariti, the Royal Court chief
best known for his anti-Saddam views, and the appointment as prime minister of Ali Abu Ragheb, a politician widely perceived as supportive of the
close economic and political relationship between Jordan and Iraq. Corre-
spondingly, Baghdad expressed its appreciation by signing a particularly
concessionary oil protocol with Jordan, by announcing plans to move ahead
on the long-discussed Baghdad–Zarqa oil pipeline, and by moving to increase Iraqi utilization of the Aqaba port. But the statistics tell the real story.
During the first five months of 1999—shortly after King Abdullah's ascension to the throne, when it was still unclear what his stance would be toward
Iraq—the Kingdom's exports to Iraq totaled 24.7 million JD. For the same
period in 2000, Jordanian exports came to 47.2 million JD.[84]

While the extent of humanitarian sympathy in Jordan for the plight of Iraqis
should not be underestimated, protocols and bilateral trade are not about compassion or charity; they are about money and influence. Iraqi officials and pro-
Iraqi Jordanians are quick to point out that Iraq provides more aid to Jordan
than does the United States. Indeed, by way of the oil protocol, Baghdad gives
Jordan between $400 million and $600 million per year. In contrast, all U.S.
aid to Jordan in 2001—economic and military—totaled $150 million.

This discrepancy is not new. As Tariq Masarweh, a Jordanian columnist for
al-Ra'i and a leading advocate for Iraq, notes, in the "past ten years, Iraq has
provided Jordan with more financial support than the U.S." The relationship
with Iraq, he says, is "a relationship of interests."[85] This sentiment is echoed by
the top leadership in Baghdad. During a speech on February 4, 2000, thanking
the Jordanian people for their ongoing support, Deputy Prime Minister Tariq
Aziz spoke of the relative advantages Iraq possesses over Jordan's other leading patron, the United States. Aziz said:

> I have heard from some Jordanian officials, who are our friends, a fact that they
> repeat; namely, that Jordan's gains from dealings with Iraq are much greater

than what the United States offers in aid. . . . All the aid Jordan gets does not equal half [of what Iraq provides]. So the Jordanian people and economy benefit from this relationship.

Aziz's comments focused on the economic assistance offered by Iraq. But implicit in his statement was a direct appeal by Baghdad to the Jordanian people to increase the pressure on their leadership to boost economic and political ties with the Iraqi regime.

This statement highlights Saddam's ability to directly influence the Jordanian people, a tactic he has employed with great success. Saddam is popular in Jordan, and from time to time he uses his popular standing to pressure the Kingdom toward more Iraq-oriented positions. In the early phase of the post-September 2000 Palestinian violence, for example, Jordanian demonstrators were said to have carried placards of the Iraqi leader during their marches. For King Abdullah, this was a not-so-subtle message that Iraq still possesses the means to foment instability in Jordan. One week later, the Jordanian prime minister set out for a visit to Baghdad.

In the final analysis, the direction of bilateral trade between Jordan and Iraq is determined by Baghdad. So while Baghdad routinely states that it is "committed to supporting the Jordanian economy,"[86] it seems apparent that the primary concern for Iraq is to maintain its strategic and economic "umbilical chord" to Amman. In the words of one Western diplomat in Amman, Jordan's continued dependence is, for Iraq, "an insurance policy in an uncertain world."[87]

NOTES

1. Abdel Salam al-Majali, interview by author, detailed notes, Amman, Jordan, October 3, 1999.

2. Muhammed Asfour, interview by author, detailed notes, Amman, Jordan, June 29, 2000.

3. Abdul Ilah al-Khatib, interview by author, detailed notes, Amman, Jordan, July 2, 2000.

4. Herbert H. Denton, "Arabs Hold Purse Strings in Jordan's Talks," *Washington Post*, April 16, 1983.

5. Laurie Brand, *Jordan's Inter-Arab Relations* (New York: Columbia University Press, 1994), 219.

6. Muhammed Asfour, interview by author, detailed notes, Amman, Jordan, June 29, 2000.

7. Bassam Badreen, "Jordan Falling Back in Love with Iraq," *Middle East Mirror*, February 3, 2000. Reports about the Saudi position on the issue of supplying oil to Jordan are often contradictory. For example, *Alexander's Gas and Oil Connections*

cited a report in *Al-Sharq al-Awsat* suggesting that Saudi Arabia had indeed offered to replace the Iraqi oil supplies. See "Jordan Committed to Buying Oil Supplies from Iraq," *Alexander's Gas and Oil Connections*, August 6, 1999.

8. Muhammed Asfour, interview by author, detailed notes, Amman, Jordan, June 29, 2000. Details of additional discussions between Asfour and Iraqi officials are cited with regard to Aqaba in note 55 of this chapter.

9. "Jordanian Foreign Minister Returns from Iraq," *Jordan Times*, December 25, 1999, in Federal Broadcast Information Service–Near East and South Asia (FBIS-NES-1999-1225), December 27, 1999.

10. While the terms of the protocols are typically released and published in the Jordanian press immediately after they are signed, copies of the actual agreements are not made available to the general public. This procedure at least raises the possibility that the announced terms of the protocols may vary slightly from the actual terms of the agreements.

11. In retrospect, the terms of the protocol were better than the actual result. In 2001, only $309 million of the $450 million in trade protocol contracts were actually implemented.

12. Tareq Ayyoub, "Government to Hike Petrol Prices to Reduce Deficit," *Jordan Times*, December 14, 2000.

13. Rana Awwad, "Kerosene Price Hiked by 21 Percent," *Jordan Times*, August 17, 2001.

14. Tareq Ayyoub, "Premier to Fly to Baghdad Wednesday," *Jordan Times*, October 31, 2000.

15. Hani Mulki, interview by author, detailed notes, Amman, Jordan, September 29, 1999.

16. Asher Susser, "Jordan," *Middle East Contemporary Survey 1984*, 525.

17. *IMF Direction of Trade Statistics Yearbook, 1992.*

18. The amounts are astronomical. Between 1996 and August 2000, the UN committee supervising the program approved some $7.71 billion worth of contracts for humanitarian supplies and over $1 billion in oil-sector-related contracts. At that time, an additional $1.789 billion in contracts was pending. UN Office of the Iraq Programme, "Weekly Update for the Period 19–25 August 2000," www.un.org/depts/oip/, August 29, 2000 [accessed February 13, 2003].

19. "Jordan, Iraq Agree to Fight Drugs, Improve Ties," *Al-Hadath*, November 1, 1999, cited in BBC Worldwide Monitoring, March 11, 1999.

20. "UN Approves $129.5 Million Worth of Jordanian Exports to Iraq," *Jordan Times*, July 31, 2000. During an interview with Iraqi minister of trade Saleh in February 2000, he said the total value of contracts signed was worth $842.2 million. See "Minister Views Trade with Jordan, Comments on Sanctions," *Al-Ra'i*, February 1, 2000, cited in BBC Summary of World Broadcasts, February 12, 2000.

21. Hani Mulki, interview by author, detailed notes, Amman, Jordan, September 29, 1999.

22. Fahd al-Fanek, "Trade Protocol with Iraq Needs Control," *Jordan Times*, November 27, 2000.

23. See appendix B for further details of the Jordanian–Iraqi ghee trade.

24. Hanan Sboul, secretary general of the Jordanian Pharmaceutical Manufacturers Association, interview by author, detailed notes, Amman, Jordan, June 27, 2000.

25. Muhammed Asfour, interview by author, detailed notes, Amman, Jordan, June 29, 2000.

26. "Pharmaceuticals Vie to Boost Exports to Iraq," *Jordan Times*, May 15, 2000.

27. Ahmad al-Shuruf, "Iraq to Import $20 Million in Medicine from Jordan," *Al-Dustur*, September 21, 1999, cited in FBIS-NES-1999-0921, September 24, 1999.

28. "Al-Iraq yrafa qima mushtariyatu min al-duwa al-Urduni ila 32 milyun dular," *Al-Ra'i*, November 6, 1999.

29. "Minister Views Trade with Jordan, Comments on Sanctions," *Al-Ra'i*, February 1, 2000, cited in BBC Summary of World Broadcasts, February 12, 2000.

30. Rana Awwad, "Jordan's Trade with Iraq 'Markedly' Improves over 1st Ten Months of 2000," *Jordan Times*, December 19, 2000, in FBIS-NES-2000-1219, December 21, 2000.

31. Tareq Ayyoub, "Jordanian Pharmaceutical Exports Rose 20 Percent in 2001," *Jordan Times*, March 7, 2002.

32. "Fi tasrihat lisafirna fi Baghdad . . . Al-Hamud: rafa qima al-brutukul al-tijari biyna al-Urdun wal-Iraq siyasahum bidafa ajlat iqtisadna al-watani," *Al-Dustur*, February 2, 1999.

33. Tahseen Shurdum, interview by author, detailed notes, Amman, Jordan, October 12, 1999.

34. "Al-Malik al-Hussein yu'alin khita litahsin al-hudud maa al-Iraq," *Al-Malaf al-Iraqi*, February 1997.

35. "Jordanian Minister on Opposition, Iraq," *Al-Majallah*, March 22–18, 1998, cited in FBIS-NES-98-085, March 27, 1998.

36. Off-the-record interview by author with a Jordanian minister, detailed notes, Amman, Jordan, October 1999.

37. Eid al-Fayez, interview by author, detailed notes, Amman, Jordan, October 2, 1999.

38. Nasr al-Lawzi, interview by author, detailed notes, Amman, Jordan, October 2, 1999.

39. See, for example, "Jordan Arrests Iraqi Man for Arms Smuggling," *Iraq Press* (Amman), November 27, 2001.

40. Khaldoun Abu Hassan, interview by author, detailed notes, Amman, Jordan, October 12, 1999.

41. Saad Hattar, "Shipping Agents Association Discusses Ways to Enhance Industry," *Jordan Times*, October 25, 2000.

42. See Paul Conlon, "How Legal Were Jordan's Oil Imports from Iraq?" *Middle East Economic Survey*, February 26, 1996. Conlon's inside account of the workings of the Sanctions Committee is the most comprehensive available. See Paul Conlon, *United Nations Sanctions Management: A Case Study of the Iraq Sanctions Committee, 1990–1994.*

43. See Conlon, also documents published by Conlon's Transjuris e.K., an international legal information and support firm in Munich, Germany.

44. Tawfiq Kawar, quoted in "UN Official and Jordanian Officials Discuss Effects of Iraq Blockage on Jordan," Jordanian Television, Amman, March 30, 1994, cited in BBC Summary of World Broadcasts, April 5, 1994.

45. Amy Kaslow, "U.S. to Pay Large Sums for Helping Jordan Make Peace with Israel," *Christian Science Monitor*, August 4, 1994. The article cites then minister of state Jawad al-Anani.

46. "Jordanian Columnist Wonders Why His Country Is Still Being Choked," *Mideast Mirror*, March 17, 1997.

47. "Lloyd's Inspections Start at Aqaba," Arab Press Service Diplomatic Recorder, August 27, 1994.

48. "Special Report on Jordan: Relief Felt as Naval Blockade Ends," *Lloyd's List*, September 26, 1994.

49. "Cargo Again Flows Freely at Jordan's Aqaba Port," *Journal of Commerce*, September 15, 1994.

50. "Jordanian Shippers Criticize Onshore Cargo Inspection Rules," *Journal of Commerce*, April 9, 1997.

51. "Qata al naql fil Urdun" (The Transportation Sector in Jordan), The Hashemite Kingdom of Jordan, Ministry of Transport, Division of Research and Studies (1998), 87.

52. Muhammed Asfour, interview by author, detailed notes, Amman, Jordan, June 29, 2000.

53. "Jordan Trade Minister's Visit to Baghdad," *Al-Dustur*, November 6, 1999, cited in FBIS-NES-1999-1106, November 20, 1999.

54. "Jordanian Trade Minister Says Visit to Iraq Very Successful," *Al-Dustur*, November 6, 1999, cited in BBC Worldwide Monitoring, August 11, 1999.

55. Muhammed Asfour, interview by author, detailed notes, Amman, Jordan, June 29, 2000. In Arabic, Asfour said: "*Ma bijuz.*"

56. Hassan Shobaki, "Jordan Considers Declining Trade with Iraq," *Jordan Times*, January 21–22, 2000.

57. See, for example, Saad Hattar, "Aqaba Port Reduces Shipment Fees of Iraq-Bound Goods," *Jordan Times*, May 9, 2000.

58. Al-Jazy Shipping and Forwarding (shipping agents), Amman, Jordan.

59. "Al-Iraq: mashru litarmim matar al-Basra wa tarkiz ala istikhdam mina al-Aqaba," *Al-Hayat*, August 2, 2000.

60. "Jordan, Iraq Seek Stronger, Wider Trade Protocol," *Jordan Times*, September 7, 2000.

61. "Al-Urdun yatlub min al-Um al-mutahida anha al-taftish ala al-bada al-Iraqiyya fi mina al-Aqaba," *Al-Hayat al-Jadida*, September 14, 2000.

62. "Al-Urdun yantahi raqaba sharika Lloyds fi mina al-Aqaba," *Al-Usbu al-Arabi*, October 30, 2000.

63. Dubai Ports Authority website, www.dpa.co.ae, 2003 [accessed February 13, 2003].

64. "Qata al-naql fil Urdun" (The Transportation Sector in Jordan), The Hashemite Kingdom of Jordan, Ministry of Transport, Division of Research and Studies (1998), 65.

65. Ahmed Nasir, "Jordanian-Iraqi Firm Seeks to Expand Land Transport Fleet," *Jordan Times*, June 30, 1998, cited in FBIS-NES-98-181, July 1, 1998.

66. "Al-Ra'is al-Masri yabhath maa na'ib al-ra'is al-Iraqi," *Al-Sharq al-Awsat*, January 18, 2001.

67. Yanal al-Bustami, interview by author, detailed notes, Amman, Jordan, October 2, 1999.

68. Munir Soubir, interview by author, detailed notes, Amman, Jordan, October 4, 1999.

69. Tawfiq Kawar, interview by author, detailed notes, Amman, Jordan, September 30, 1999.

70. Hani Mulki, interview by author, detailed notes, Amman, Jordan, September 29, 1999.

71. Laith al-Qassem, interview by author, detailed notes, Amman, Jordan, October 6, 1999. This happens on a government-to-government basis as well. In the mid-1990s, for example, on completing $100,000 worth of maintenance on Syrian airplanes, the Central Bank of Syria informed Royal Jordanian that they had no dollars and hence would pay Royal Jordanian in Syrian lira.

72. "Peace in the Middle East and the Jordanian Economy," prepared text of remarks delivered by Rima Khalaf-Hunaidi at the Washington Institute for Near East Policy, September 30, 1999.

73. United Nations Conference on Trade and Development, "Cooperation between the Palestinian Authority, Egypt and Jordan to Enhance Subregional Trade-Related Services," February 14, 2000. See UNCTAD, www.unctad.org, 2002 [accessed February 13, 2003].

74. Tareq Ayyoub, "Controversy over Jordan-Israeli Trade Figures," *Jordan Times*, August 16, 2002.

75. "Anti-normalization Committee Member Released on Bail," Petra News, February 13, 2001, cited in BBC Summary of World Broadcasts, February 15, 2001. One of the cited officials was Chief of the Royal Court Fayez Tarawneh. Anti-Normalization Committee head Ali Abu Sukar and several others were subsequently imprisoned for publishing this list despite repeated warnings from the Jordanian government.

76. "Lajnat muqawamat al-tatbi badaa'at tahrihatha: Al-Iraq yarfud safqat li sharikat duwa'iyya Urduniyya lita'amalha maa Israel," *Al-Dustur*, March 22, 1999.

77. Marwan al-Qassem, interview by author, detailed notes, Amman, Jordan, June 29, 2000.

78. "Ashadat bijuhud al-wafd al-Urduni al-mufawad: al-Fa'aliyat al-iqtisadiyya tu'akid ahamiyya maa tam injazuh fi Bagdhad," *Al-Dustur*, January 24, 2000.

79. Mwrawid al-Tel, interview by author, detailed notes, Amman, Jordan, October 7, 1999.

80. "Ashadat bijuhud al-wafd al-Urduni al-mufawad: al-Fa'aliyat al-iqtisadiyya tu'akid ahamiyya maa tam injazuh fi Bagdhad," *Al-Dustur*, January 24, 2000.

81. Eid al-Fayez, interview by author, detailed notes, Amman, Jordan, October 2, 1999.

82. This view is held by the top echelon of Jordanian economic officials. Ahmed Abdel Fatteh, then deputy governor of the Central Bank of Jordan, was one such example.

83. Judith Miller, "CIA Is Said to Find Iraq Gives Contracts to Nations That Want to End Economic Sanctions," *New York Times*, September 7, 2000.

84. *Jordan Economic Monitor* (a monthly newsletter published and edited by Dr. Fahed al-Fanek), August 2000. In the same period, Jordanian imports from Iraq more than doubled as well, from 91.2 million JD to 194.8 million JD.

85. Tariq Masarweh, interview by author, detailed notes, Amman, Jordan, October 11, 1999.

86. See, for example, comments by Iraqi minister of trade Muhammed Mehdi Salih in "Iraqi Minister Hails Increase of Trade with Jordan," *Al-Dustur*, January 31, 2000, cited in BBC Summary of World Broadcasts, February 5, 2000.

87. Interview with a Western diplomat in Jordan who travels frequently between Amman and Baghdad, detailed notes, Amman, Jordan, June 28, 2000.

Chapter Three

Pro-Iraq Elements in Jordan

Given their geographic proximity, economic interdependence, and intertwined histories, it is not surprising that Jordan and Iraq frequently interfere in each other's domestic affairs. This interference has included King Hussein's 1995 call for the removal of Saddam Hussein, and Saddam's periodic calls for the overthrow of the "dwarfs" ruling Amman. In the decade since the 1991 Gulf War, fishing in the troubled waters of Amman and Baghdad has been a favorite pastime of both Iraqi and Jordanian rulers, respectively. But whereas Jordan today has almost no influence in Baghdad, Iraq—despite more than ten years of UN economic sanctions—holds a preponderance of both political and economic sway in Jordan.

Saddam's influence has not come by accident. Since 1979, he has cultivated, bullied, and/or purchased a considerable degree of support within Jordan and, in so doing, developed a hard core of support for Iraq among Jordanians. Collectively, this Iraq "lobby" has proved the leading advocate for Iraqi interests in Jordan. What follows is a discussion of some of these organizations and their activities.

THE IRAQ LOBBY

Over the years, Saddam has cultivated a strong base of support among Jordanian intellectuals, businessmen, journalists, and politicians of both Arab nationalist and Islamist stripes. Whereas humanitarian support for Iraqis is genuine, some of the political support appears to have been acquired by less honorable means.

Saddam's campaign to win hearts and minds in Jordan traces back to 1979, when, in the aftermath of ambitious Arab Summit financial commitments

made to "frontline" states like Jordan, Iraq was one of the few states to fulfill
its obligations. Years later, Saddam bought and paid for the 1987 Amman
Arab Summit, where the major achievement was an Arab reaffirmation of
Iraqi rights vis-à-vis Iran.

Perhaps more that any other means, though, Saddam succeeded in cultivating a base of support among Jordanian elites via an elaborate system of financial rewards, bribes, incentives, and patronage payoffs issued to his parti-
sans in the Kingdom.

In 1991, an article in the *Wall Street Journal* described how Saddam had
donated $3 million to a journalists' "housing fund" in Amman—used by edi-
tors and reporters to finance their homes—presumably in exchange for positive coverage in the Jordanian press.[1] Saddam's attempts to cultivate support
via the media have not been confined to Jordan. Indeed, Egyptian writer
Yusef Idris noted to the *Journal* that "half of Saddam's efforts over the years
have been devoted to courting the mass media" throughout the Arab world.
Reports have even surfaced that Saddam has established a pro-Iraq lobby
among influential "political and military" circles in Russia.[2]

In 1995, the pan-Arab newspaper *al-Hayat* ran a series of articles by Amman correspondent Salameh Ne'matt about the Iraq lobby in Jordan. Most notably, an article citing a well-placed source warned that Iraqi parties were re-
cruiting in order to "shape the trend" against the official Jordanian position,
which, in the aftermath of the Hussein Kamel defection, was turning against
Iraq. The article mentioned a list of forty-two prominent "writers, journalists,
and a number of high-ranking current and former officials, among them current government ministers, all on Saddam's payroll."[3]

Evidently, these assertions reflected just the tip of the proverbial iceberg.
In subsequent publications and radio appearances, Ne'matt made additional
allegations that painted a fuller picture of how Iraq purchased influence in
Jordan. He discussed how sons of prominent Jordanian politicians received
lucrative contracts with Iraq, either via Oil for Food or through other mecha-
nisms. Ne'matt also spoke about government officials on the Iraqi "take,"
some of whom were given gratuities of new homes or Mercedes Benz sedans.
According to Ne'matt, in 1990 Saddam offered forty-two cars "as gifts" to
ministers in the government of Mudar Badran.

Ne'matt's favorite topic, however, was the Jordanian media establishment,
and he did not shy away from naming individuals and companies paid by
Saddam for favorable coverage. He described, for example, how the Jordanian daily *al-Dustur* was awarded a plush $2 million contract to publish "cul-
tural books" from the Iraqi government.[4] He likewise cited several colum-
nists, intellectuals, and newspaper editors who comprised the core of the Iraqi
lobby in Jordan.

Although the Iraq lobby is frequently discussed in Amman, few Jordanian informants—other than Ne'matt himself—would speak about the topic on the record. The fear of reprisal is real and compelling. Given that his information was independently corroborated by other reliable journalists—Ne'matt says that his informant was Hussein Kamel himself—his short list is at least worth mentioning. Some of the most influential people cited by Ne'matt include: Riyad Hurub, editor of the newspaper *Arab al-Yawm*; Fahd al-Fanek, economic columnist for *al-Ra'i* and its sister publication, the *Jordan Times;* Tariq Masarweh, former spokesman of the Jordanian Royal Court and *al-Ra'i* columnist; and Hani Khasawneh, former minister of information, chief of royal protocol, and *al-Ra'i* columnist.

Significantly, the writings of these men do not stand out as the most stridently pro-Iraq commentaries in Jordan. In fact, these commentators would likely describe themselves as "pan-Arab nationalists," who feel that it is appropriate to defend Iraq from its detractors. Over the years, however, the positions that they have advocated in support of Iraq have been remarkably consistent, even on issues where other traditionally pro-Iraqi journalists have been critical. Both Tariq Masarweh and Fahd al-Fanek, for example, applauded the 1997 executions of the four Jordanians in Iraq accused of smuggling auto parts. Likewise, in 1998 Masarweh ruled out the possibility of any Iraqi involvement in the Ma'an bread riots, instead placing unequivocal blame on the U.S. military buildup to Operation Desert Fox.[5]

Masarweh, who paid a get-well visit to Saddam's son Uday after he was injured in an unsuccessful assassination attempt, sharply criticized Hussein Kamel for his defection. Masarweh even suggested that the shootings of Israeli diplomats in Amman shortly after the outbreak of the Palestinian uprising were the work of the Mossad.

For his part, Fahd al-Fanek's writings have advocated a restoration of ties to Iraq based primarily on economic rationale. As part of this program, he called in 1997 for the expulsion "not tomorrow but today" of Lloyd's Register.[6] (Three years later, Lloyd's Aqaba inspection operation was permanently closed by King Abdullah.) Following Prime Minster Ali Abu Ragheb's historic visit to Baghdad in November 2000, Fanek expressed his appreciation to Saddam and the people of Iraq "who deserve freedom and democracy as soon as the siege is lifted."[7]

Since leaving government in the late 1980s, one-time Jordanian minister of information Hani Khasawneh has emerged as an outspoken proponent of Iraq and a peddler of conspiracy theories. He maintains that the Hussein Kamel affair was fabricated[8] and said during a 1999 speech that the embargo on Iraq was "proof of the Zionist conspiracy against the Arab community [*umma*]."[9] Not surprisingly, Khasawneh denies the existence of an Iraq lobby in Jordan, a phenomenon he claims is "the work of intelligence services," to "confuse the genuine feelings toward Iraq" in the Kingdom.[10] Educated in Iraq and Cairo in the 1960s and a former member of the Ba'th party, Khasawneh makes no effort to conceal his own genuine feelings toward Saddam, whom he considers a "friend."[11]

All told, it has been alleged that the Iraq lobby controls more than four major Jordanian dailies and a news service. The result, said a prominent journalist in Amman who preferred to remain anonymous, is that "very few journalists will write negative stories" about Iraq.

ASSOCIATION INVOLVEMENT

In addition to journalists, the pro-Iraq public relations campaign in the Kingdom has been assisted by a broad range of professional associations and unions as well as Islamist personalities like Abdul Munem Abu Zant and Laith Shubeilat, who are likewise said to have been on the Iraqi payroll.

The Jordanian Bar Association provides a good example of the extent to which these groups are involved in the Iraq issue. Led by Saleh Armouti (who was elected in April 1999), the association has been a high-profile proponent in the crusade to terminate UN sanctions on Iraq. For several months in 2000 after an Italian pilot illegally flew from Jordan to Baghdad, the association tried to organize its own sanctions-busting flight. To accomplish this, the group attempted to rent a private airplane, "not to take donations to Iraq, but to break the air embargo imposed on it."[12]

While Armouti's organization is perhaps the most prominent of the professional associations involved in efforts to end sanctions against Iraq, dozens of other groups also play a role. In April 2000, following the example of the Bar Association, the Jordanian Construction Contractors Association attempted to organize an embargo-breaking flight to Baghdad as a show of "solidarity." Some months later, the Agricultural Associations Council, which represents several groups including the Fruit and Vegetable Exporters and Producers Association as well as the Jordan Farmers Union, organized a similar solidarity flight.

In addition to the proliferation of illegal flights, professional associations have attempted to institute boycotts against American products to protest U.S. policy. In the aftermath of Operation Desert Fox in 1998, for example, the various associations representing doctors, geologists, nurses, journalists, engineers, pharmacists, artists, and writers called on Jordanians to eschew all activities organized by the U.S. and British embassies in Amman. At about the same time, the Jordan Medical Association and the Pharmacists Association urged a blacklist of American and British medical products. In February 1999, Iraq played host to a large gathering of professional unions. The Jordanian delegation—with some eighty representatives—was the largest delegation in attendance.[13] During the meeting, the Jordanian Health Association renewed its public call for a general Arab boycott of U.S.- and British-made medical products.[14]

One of the more striking examples of the fervor with which the professional associations support Iraq came in December 1998, following Operation Desert Fox. During a rally at Jordan University protesting the bombings, representatives of Jordan's trade unions announced that they had sent a letter to UN secretary general Kofi Annan threatening retaliation. The letter stated: "Our people are left with no other choice but to fight back—terrorism should be paid back in kind . . . if they kill our people today by their tomahawks and their British Tornadoes, let them be sure that their blood and life shall be shed with no second thoughts."[15]

AMMAN CHAMBER OF INDUSTRY:
THE PREEMINENT PRO-IRAQ LOBBY

The most powerful institution in Jordan today promoting increased trade with Iraq is the Amman Chamber of Industry (ACI). Established in 1962, ACI is a nongovernmental organization representing Jordan's industrial sector. Widely recognized as the driving force in Jordan's trade policy, it has also served as the leading advocate in Jordan for increased economic ties to Iraq.

One of ACI's primary concerns is Jordan's "export orientation."[16] ACI exerts influence on Jordanian economic planning via its members' participation in influential government economic institutions as well as by the frequent participation of its members in top-level meetings between Jordanian and Iraqi officials. The chamber also directly lobbies the Iraqi government for increased bilateral trade. In fact, under the leadership of former chairman Khaldoun Abu Hassan, who until 1991 served as chairman of the Royal Jordanian Airlines—ACI played an active role in negotiating most of the Jordanian—Iraqi trade protocols from 1996 through 2000.

More than just serving as a lobbyist for improved Jordanian–Iraqi relations, however, ACI has played an important role in developing Iraqi–Arab relations. An ardent nationalist and public critic of Jordan–Israel peace, Abu Hassan used his position at the chamber to encourage not only a Jordanian economic rapprochement with Iraq but the political and economic reintegration of Iraq into the region as well. Indeed, Abu Hassan maintains that ACI has served as the "conduit of relations" between Iraqi business and the Arab world.[17] In addition to these projects, many of ACI's activities are focused on ending the sanctions against Iraq, which the organization claims is actually a "blockade on Jordan."[18]

Not surprisingly, given its goals, the chamber has in recent years been disappointed with the low level of the bilateral trade protocols. The leadership typically expresses moderate praise when the government raises a protocol, but without exception expresses disappointment at what it considers small, incremental increases. In recent years, the chamber has pressed for an annual doubling of the protocols in an effort to return to the levels of the early 1990s.[19]

During an October 1999 interview, Abu Hassan described the role of the chamber. Quite simply, he stated: "We are . . . the strongest economic lobby for Iraq" in Jordan.[20] It is not difficult to see why. During his tenure as ACI chairman, Abu Hassan was a frequent visitor to Baghdad, leading high-profile trade missions to the Iraqi capital four times per year. While in Iraq, Abu Hassan operated in a quasi-official capacity, meeting regularly with Iraqi trade ministers, vice presidents, and occasionally with Saddam himself. When in Baghdad, he was treated as a virtual head of state.

ACI delegations to Baghdad introduce a broad range of Jordanian industrialists seeking trade contracts with Iraq to the right people. During one such mission in September 1999, Abu Hassan was in the Iraqi capital for discussions with government officials as well as heads and members of the Iraqi Chambers of Industry and Trade on expanding Jordan's exports to Iraq. The delegation included representatives of companies producing plastics, paper, printing, detergents, vegetable oil, cosmetics, foodstuffs, medicines, construction materials, wooden doors, school equipment, and boilers for hospitals.[21]

For the chamber, one of the most important events on the calendar is the annual Baghdad International Trade Fair. This large fair in 2000—970 companies from thirty-eight countries attended—provided a good opportunity for companies to display their wares to Iraqi consumers. Jordan's representation is organized by ACI, and the leader of the delegation is generally the chamber's chairman. Jordanian corporate turnout is typically very good; in 1998, sixty-six local companies attended the event, and in 2000 the Jordanian contingent had its own "wing" at the fair.

In addition to establishing business contacts for Jordanian industrialists in Baghdad, it seems that one of the main missions of ACI is to keep bilateral trade issues with Iraq in the public spotlight. To this end, ACI leaders are constantly featured in the Jordanian press talking about the need to increase trade with Iraq. As part of its ongoing activities, ACI also hosts top Iraqi officials for meetings and discussions.[22]

On May 12, 2000, the Amman Chamber of Industry went to the polls and voted to replace longtime chairman Khaldoun Abu Hassan with the well-respected businessman Othman Bdeir. Some Jordanians cried foul, suggesting that Abu Hassan lost because of unprecedented government intervention in the elections.[23] While the government decision to move the site of ACI polling was odd, there does not appear to be further evidence of election irregularities. Insiders suggest that Abu Hassan was not brought down by a conspiracy, but rather that he "overstayed his welcome and was mistrusted by colleagues because of self-aggrandizement."

If Bdeir's stated platform is any indication, he is less protectionist and more supportive of economic reform than his predecessor.[24] On the issue of Israel, Bdeir, too, is on record as opposing "normalization." Despite the other minor differences in platform, however, it appears that on the issue of Iraq, there will be continuity in ACI leadership. Like Abu Hassan, Othman Bdeir and his party believe that Iraq is Jordan's most important market.

NATIONAL MOBILIZATION COMMITTEE
FOR THE DEFENSE OF IRAQ

The most prominent public organization in the matrix of Jordanian groups dedicated to ending UN sanctions has been the National Mobilization Committee for the Defense of Iraq (NMCDI). The activities of NMCDI—an amalgam of representatives from political parties, unions and federations, the Muslim Brotherhood, and other pro-Iraq political activists—have focused on raising public awareness and lobbying the Kingdom's politicians. In addition to sending several public letters to Jordan's prime minister and parliament speaker, NMCDI initiated a petition-writing campaign and several nationwide collection drives to dispatch goods to Iraq. In May 2000, for example, NMCDI submitted an open petition to parliament with fifty-eight thousand signatures—over 1 percent of the population—demanding that the legislature pressure the government to "announce its rebellion against the continued prohibitive economic resolutions on Iraq and salvage the embargoed Jordanian national economy."[25] The petition also requested that Jordan resume its air links with Iraq and end the role of Lloyd's Register in supervising transit through Aqaba.

The most celebrated initiative of NMCDI has been its Pencil Campaign. Though the origin of the rumor is uncertain, Jordanians and Iraqis somehow came to believe that lead pencils were among the list of items not permitted for export to Iraq under the UN sanctions regime.[26] Because of this allegedly pernicious UN policy, Iraqi school children were said to be facing a terrible shortage of pencils. Although there is no indication that the UN ever prohibited the entry of pencils into Iraq—in fact, according to the UN "Basic Figures" sheet, phase eight of the Oil-for-Food program allocated some $389 million for education[27]—some Jordanians seized on this rumor to begin a well-publicized "humanitarian" campaign in 1999 to provide Iraqi children with the pencils they needed.

Over the course of two months, NMCDI gathered over 3 million pencils, mostly donated by average Jordanians. It was, according to campaign spokesperson Aida Dabbas, "a frenzy." By late January 2000, the pencils were loaded onto trucks and driven to Baghdad, where the convoy was greeted with a rousing reception. Addressing the crowd, Iraqi deputy prime minister Tariq Aziz praised NMCDI and the Jordanian people for siding with the people of Iraq and mocked the alleged UN prohibition on pencils, asking derisively, "How many pencils will Iraq need to put these graphics [*sic*] together and make a missile?"[28] Hamza Mansour, a leader of both the Jordanian Muslim Brotherhood and NMCDI, explained to Iraqi television the rationale of the pencil campaign: "We are certain that the blockade will not be lifted by virtue of a resolution issued by the UN, which has now become subordinate to the U.S. State Department. Therefore, it is impossible to cancel this blockade or end it. Only through breaking it can this embargo be lifted."[29]

ISLAMIST ADVOCACY ON BEHALF OF IRAQ

Although readily apparent, it bears mentioning that solidarity with Iraq is at the top of the political agenda of Jordanian Islamists. Driven by the perceived suffering of fellow Muslims, Jordan's Muslim Brotherhood has been at the forefront of campaigns to raise funds and collect goods for the Iraqi people. Its leaders often participate in "solidarity" missions to Baghdad, where they meet with Iraqi leaders and express their comradeship in the face of Western "aggression." Likewise, Iraq—Saddam in particular—represents the continued struggle against Israel, a struggle that Jordan since 1994 has officially abandoned. In this sense, although many Islamists consider the regime in Iraq to be both repressive and regressive, the latter still merits their support. Finally, for many Islamists in Jordan, Iraq constitutes a powerful symbol of defiance of Western hegemony at a time when the Hashemite leadership seems fully in the Western/American camp. Indeed, support for Iraq is the rare issue on which the Islamists sometimes find themselves making common cause with the Jordanian government. For example, in November 2000, not long after the Islamist press lambasted the government for expelling Hamas leaders from Jordan, the same newspapers heaped praise on the Jordanian leadership for sending Prime Minister Ali Abu Ragheb to meet with Saddam in Baghdad.[30]

STUDENTS

While humanitarian concerns, political affinity, and economic interest are the proximate reasons for the close Jordanian connection to Iraq, the Jordanian elite have an even more personal reason to feel the bond with Baghdad: a sizable percentage spent a formative period of their lives in the Iraqi capital. Indeed, Iraq has traditionally been the Arab country to which Jordanians travel to attend university. Because Jordan had no public university system until 1962, two generations of Jordanians had to seek university and professional training abroad, and Iraq was the prime destination. Even after 1962, Jordanian students continued to choose Iraq as one of their most preferred locations for foreign study.

There are several reasons why Jordanian students sought out Iraqi universities. Long recognized as perhaps the most technologically advanced Arab state, Iraq built institutions of higher education considered among the finest in the Arab world. Iraq's oil wealth also gave it the resources to extend subsidies to Jordanians and other Arab students, offering prized opportunities for a top-quality education at rock-bottom prices. While Nasser's Egypt also attracted numerous Jordanian students in the 1950s and 1960s, Cairo eventually instituted financial requirements (including mandatory exchange transactions at the "official" rate) that proved too expensive for many Jordanians. By default, Baghdad became the foreign "college town" of choice.

By the 1980s, about five thousand Jordanians attended college and university in Iraq each year, comprising about 10 percent of Jordan's total higher education enrollment. Among this number were many of the top echelon of Jordan's decision makers today (e.g., the chairman and deputy chairman of Jordan's Central Bank are both alumni of Iraqi universities). Jordanian enrollment in Iraq declined in the 1990s, apparently due to the worsening living conditions in Iraq. By the end of the decade, about equal numbers of Jordanians—approximately three thousand each—were studying in universities in Iraq, Syria, and Lebanon.[31]

Perhaps because undergraduate education is better in Baghdad, few Iraqi students come to Jordan for four-year degrees. Of the 10,651 foreign undergraduates enrolled in Jordanian institutions in 1997–1998, only 403 were Iraqi.[32] By comparison, 732 Syrian students attended Jordanian universities that academic year. Interestingly, although the numbers are significantly lower, Iraqi graduate students appear to have some preference for Jordan. That same year, Iraqi students comprised one-quarter—184 of 725—of all registered foreign graduate students studying in the Kingdom.[33] Syria, by contrast, had just 15 registered graduate students in Jordan that year. Table 3.1 shows how many Jordanian students studied abroad and in Iraq in the 1980s and 1990s.

From time to time, it appears that Saddam employs the Jordanian students studying in Iraq for propaganda purposes. In September 1995, for example, the Baghdad branch of the General Union of Jordanian Students

Table 3.1.   Jordanian Students Studying Abroad and Studying in Iraq, 1986–1999

Years	Total # Abroad	Total # Iraq	B.A. Stud.	M.A. Stud.	Ph.D. Stud.
86–87	36,019	1,325	1,297*	4	0
87–88	34,459	1,560	1,550	10	0
88–89	33,566	No info	No info	No info	No info
89–90	32,817	1,363	1,363	0	0
90–91	35,934	No info	No info	No info	No info
91–92	35,034	No info	No info	No info	No info
92–93	31,943	1,337	1,322	11	4
93–94	32,500	1,218	1,194	20	4
94–95	30,928	2,094	2,056	29	9
95–96	29,581	No info	No info	No info	No info
96–97	33,170	4,392	4,200	108	32
97–98	29,696	2,984	2,736	140	108
98–99	21,084	2,984	2,736	140	108

*Technical and/or Associate's Degree.
Numbers from the Jordanian Ministry of Higher Education.

sent a public cable to the Iraqi leader affirming the glorious role of Iraq in maintaining the "dignity and honor" of the Arab nation. The cable also said that the students were "aware of the true nature of the conspiracy being hatched by the imperialist and Zionist circles against Arab aspirations."[34] Likewise, the Association of Jordanian Students in Iraq, housed in a large building in downtown Amman, is active in promoting Iraqi causes and encouraging more students to choose Iraq for their studies. All this is not to suggest that Jordanian students returning from Iraq are "tools" of Saddam. But after four years in Baghdad, these students usually seem to return home with a special fondness for Iraqis. This was particularly the case from the 1950s through the 1980s, when Amman was looked on as a provincial capital, while Baghdad was seen as a "real city." Middle-aged Jordanian alumni of Iraqi universities often look back on their days in Baghdad with misty-eyed nostalgia. While it is impossible to quantify how this personal connection effects decision making in Amman, it is another important tie that binds the two societies together.

CHARGES BROUGHT AGAINST NE'MATT FOR THE "IRAQ LOBBY" ARTICLES

The revelations published in Salameh Ne'matt's 1995 series of *al-Hayat* articles touched off a firestorm in Amman. The regime retaliated by arresting

Ne'matt and charging him with the crimes of "threatening Jordanian national unity" (i.e., promoting *fitna*, or chaos), "slandering the Government," and "violating the Press and Publications Law" (i.e., inaccurate reporting)—crimes that could carry prison terms of up to seven years for each conviction.[35] The arraignment occurred during one of King Hussein's trips abroad. During this procedure, Ne'matt was ordered to reveal his informants, but he refused, instead claiming his rights under the Press and Publications Law. In response, the government prosecutor remanded him to two weeks in Juweida prison. On learning of this decree, King Hussein evidently telephoned his brother, Hassan, then acting as regent, and ordered Ne'matt's release. When the trial resumed, it garnered media attention around the Arab world, with *al-Hayat*'s editor, Jihad al-Khazen, even flying to Amman to testify on his employee's behalf. After a six-month trial, Ne'matt was acquitted—or, as Ne'matt described it, "vindicated."

Even so, the trial had a chilling effect on any critical media coverage of Iraq in Jordan. Ne'matt's trial had begun in December 1995 against the backdrop of the arrival earlier that year of Hussein Kamel. Already, the Iraq lobby in Jordan was working overtime to control the damage from Kamel's defection and King Hussein's support for political change in Baghdad. The fact that the lobby could succeed in convincing the government to try Ne'matt on blatantly trumped up charges, even if it could not win a conviction, was enough to silence any other journalist from writing about the powerful web of interests that worked inside Jordan on behalf of the Iraqi regime.

THE ANTI-IRAQ LOBBY?

According to Iraqi minister of trade Muhammad Mahdi Saleh, "There is a lobby inside of Jordan working to destroy the relations with Iraq."[36] This group, he says, "works day and night agitating against Iraq." Jordanian commentator and renowned Iraq supporter Fahd al-Fanek agrees. "The lobby exists," he says. "It is known as the 'Kabariti lobby.'"[37]

Throughout a career that has combined private business with public service, Abdel Karim al-Kabariti has proven a controversial personality. A reformer who supports economic liberalization and modernization of the Jordanian economy, Kabariti has also been an outspoken advocate of domestic political reform. In fact, it was in 1996, during his tenure as prime minister, that Kabariti became the first such incumbent ever to meet with the heads of Jordanian political parties.

In all these reformist efforts, Kabariti was never afraid to ruffle feathers, at times infuriating both royals and commoners alike. Few targets were immune: he was celebrated (or infamous) for cutting bread subsidies to the poor and slashing the budget of the Royal Court. Kabariti's detractors—of whom there are many—say that he is personally abrasive and politically counter-productive, pushing an agenda that they argue is contrary to Jordan's best interests. A top complaint against Kabariti has been what his critics consider to be his bias against Iraq.

Indeed, Kabariti has never concealed his distaste for Saddam and the Ba'thist ruling clique in Baghdad. In 1996, he went so far as to describe Iraq as a "big prison."[38] His vocal advocacy on behalf of Kuwaiti prisoners of war and MIAs from the 1990 Iraqi invasion of Kuwait has also made him a long-time irritant for Iraq. Given his antipathy toward Saddam's regime, it is not surprising that Kabariti's government pursued policies that aroused Baghdad's ire. During his tenure as foreign minister, for example, Jordan allowed the Iraqi opposition group Iraqi National Accord (INA) to open an office in Amman. Likewise, in 1996 Kabariti succeeded in purging from the government a handful of brazen pro-Iraqi apologists, including the then minister of interior as well as the chief of the Royal Court. In addition to lending tacit Jordanian support to the Iraqi opposition, Kabariti accused Iraq of interfering in the domestic affairs of the Kingdom. Following the August 1996 bread riots, Kabariti's government expelled a diplomat serving at the Iraqi embassy in Amman.

Iraq rarely hesitated to express its displeasure with Kabariti and his governments. In 1997, Saddam himself described Kabariti's cabinet as an "ignorant government that does not deal with matters in a presidential or understandable manner."[39] There were also rumors that year that the holdup in the signing of the annual oil protocol was an attempt by Baghdad to engineer Kabariti's ouster from the prime ministry. Though Kabariti resigned as chief of the Royal Court in early January 2000, he once again made the news that August. In the aftermath of the Jordanian–Iraqi economic rapprochement, Jordan had petitioned Baghdad to open a branch of the Jordan–Kuwait Bank in the Iraqi capital. Iraq refused, however, citing the fact that Kabariti was then serving as bank vice president.

In addition to his numerous critics in Baghdad, Kabariti has detractors in Amman, many of whom are considered to be card-carrying members of Jordan's Iraq lobby. These local critics have savaged Kabariti for his allegedly intimate ties with Israel, his alleged lack of compassion for Iraqi children, and for ignoring what they believe to be an economic imperative for closer Jordanian–Iraqi relations. For example, in September 1995, eleven Jordanian opposition parties, including the Islamic Action Front (IAF) and the Ba'th Party, signed a statement condemning Kabariti's position on Iraq. Popular Islamist Laith Shubeilat accused Kabariti of supporting the U.S. political alliance in the Gulf against Iraq and of cooperation with the Zionists.[40]

Pro-Iraq commentator Fahd al-Fanek went even further. He described a "Kabariti lobby," which he maintained was "paid by outside parties." Its goal, he said, was the "satisfaction of the Gulf states and the West."[41] According to Fanek, this Kabariti lobby works "against everything Arab, Muslim, and humanitarian."

Still other Jordanians condemn Kabariti for what they consider to be a myopic economic view of bilateral relations with Baghdad. These critics reason that given the Kingdom's perennial economic woes, existing ties with Iraq must be fully exploited. As one businessman with close ties to Baghdad confided, "Iraq is an economic power. This is a reality. Kabariti puts his head in the sand."

Despite these and other attacks, Kabariti's stand toward Iraq has been remarkably consistent with his overall worldview. Kabariti describes his policy toward Iraq—indeed, his approach to foreign policy in general—in terms of enabling Jordan to "deal with the region and the world confidently." In a 1997 interview, Kabariti outlined the four guiding principles of his government's policy:

> My government proceeded on the basis of a number of major principles. The most important of these principles are the need for self-reliance, putting Jordan's national interests above all other considerations, further enhancement of civil liberties, and establishment of balanced relations with all states of the region.[42]

Creating self-reliance, balancing relations, and putting Jordan "first" are wise policy recommendations for a weak state surrounded by powerful and hostile entities. These policy principles make sense for Jordan, a state that seeks to capitalize on its unique competitive advantage, that is, the ability to truck simultaneously with Syria, Iraq, and Israel. Kabariti's prescriptions are applicable across the board, but they are no doubt particularly appropriate for Jordanian–Iraqi relations, where a relative imbalance of ties has, at times, threatened to skew the regional equilibrium.

Clearly, Kabariti has been aware of the damage that might accompany a tilt of political disposition in Amman. He is a realist, and, as such, the policies he has advocated toward Baghdad reflect a strong skepticism of Iraqi intentions. In Jordan, where nearly a decade after the Gulf War the message of Saddam continues to resonate, Kabariti's positions have made him a controversial figure. Still, this worldview has made him a favorite of both King Hussein and his son King Abdullah (but not a favorite, one needs to add, of Prince Hassan, with whom Kabariti has been on bad terms for many years). Indeed, since 1990, Kabariti has served in some official capacity—from prime minister to minister of labor—no less than a total of six years, no small feat in the Kingdom. These years of service, including in the key role of chief of the Royal Court in King Abdullah's early months on the throne, reflect an appreciation within the ruling family of the potential threat Iraq continues to pose.

IRAQI MANIPULATION OF JORDANIAN AFFAIRS

Iraqi interference in Jordan's domestic affairs has a long and sordid history. Over the past decade, Iraq has both instigated riots and has been implicated in the assassinations of Iraqis on Jordanian soil. Baghdad has also been active in cultivating ties with, and at times manipulating individuals and trends in, the Jordanian opposition. So active has Iraq been in Jordanian internal affairs that when nefarious events occur in the Kingdom, with or without evidence, Saddam is typically singled out as the usual suspect. The example of Imad Alawi is a case in point.

In November 1998, Alawi—the brother of Iyad Alawi, the London-based leader of the Iraqi opposition group, the Iraqi National Accord—was found dead in his Amman villa. Jordanian authorities announced that the deceased was found with a single bullet in his head and quickly produced not one but three suicide notes.[43] Nevertheless, rumors persisted that Iraqi henchmen were responsible for the hit. Iyad Alawi questioned the accuracy of the Jordanian autopsy report. After all, he said, "there were two bullets in his [Imad's] head. It would be the first time anyone committing suicide has managed to shoot himself twice."[44]

One important reason why Saddam has such an extensive reach into Jordan is the large number of Iraqis who reside in the Kingdom. While it is all but certain that the Jordanian minister of the interior possesses a census or a survey detailing the exact number of Iraqis residing in Jordan, definitive statistics have never been made public. In fact, in a country that considers any demographic data to be a closely guarded state secret, information concerning the resident Iraqi population is a topic only slightly less sensitive than the number of Palestinians living in the Kingdom.

As a result, it is difficult to ascertain exactly how many Iraqis live in Jordan. Officials at the U.S. embassy in Amman peg the number at between 150,000 and 180,000. This assessment appears to be based on a 1998 pronouncement from the minister of the interior placing the number at 140,000. When this figure is modified according to departure and arrival information (kept by the Central Bank of Jordan), the number reaches about 180,000. Unofficially, however, many Western diplomats in Amman suggest that the real number is much higher. No one really knows with any degree of certainty because, as then minister of the interior Nathir Rashid admitted in a 1998 interview, "Iraqis enter Jordan as if they were going into their country without the need for them to produce passports."[45]

The problem of reaching an accurate assessment is illustrated by an interview conducted with Jordanian minister of labor Eid al-Fayez in October 1999. When queried about Iraqis in Jordan, the minister—whose ministry is responsible for tracking the Iraqi workforce in the Kingdom—initially suggested that there were only 30,000 Iraqis. A few moments later, on further reflection, he revised his initial estimate to 70,000. When further pressed by the interviewer about what appeared to be a very low estimate, the minister's adviser interrupted and reported that, indeed, there were probably more like 120,000 Iraqis in the Kingdom.[46] Other knowledgeable Jordanians offer completely different figures. Former minister of trade and industry Muhammed Asfour, for example, said there were more than 300,000 Iraqis in Jordan in 1999.[47] First secretary of the Amman Chamber of Commerce Yanal al-Bustami said he believes there are 400,000.[48]

Of course, Iraqis constitute only a fragment of the total number of expatriate laborers in Jordan. In addition to the Iraqi population, according to the pan-Arab daily *al-Hayat*, Jordan was home to some 400,000 Egyptians, 130,000 Syrians, and tens of thousands of Sudanese, Lebanese, and Pakistanis as of 1999.[49]

INTEGRATION?

Iraqis in Jordan differ from their fellow expatriate workers in that they are generally better educated and more integrated into Jordanian society. Although some reports suggest that there was an effort in 1996 to establish UN-sponsored "camps" for Iraqi refugees, these never materialized.[50] The Iraqi workforce in Jordan consists mostly of professionals, not agricultural day laborers, as with the large cohort of Egyptians. Many observers point out that in addition to filling many positions in the education system, the Iraqi presence has been a boon to the world of arts, music, and literature in the Kingdom. An August 7, 2001, *Jordan Times* article titled "Local Art Scene Eclipsed by Iraqi Artists" is indicative of the phenomenon.

Interestingly, the influx of so many qualified foreign workers into an already tight Jordanian labor market has encouraged a backlash. In September 2000, for example, Jordanian doctoral graduates, who have faced great difficultly finding work in the Kingdom, protested that state universities in Jordan employed as lecturers nine hundred non-Jordanian Ph.D.s, including many Iraqis.[51] Typically, these foreign academics receive lower pay than do Jordanian nationals.

While the arrival of a few hundred thousand Iraqis has benefited Jordanian arts, some critics whisper that the presence of this large expatriate community has had a pernicious effect on the values and nature of Jordanian society. As one local observer noted, "The trend [in Jordanian society] is definitely in the wrong direction," particularly with regard to crime, drugs, abandoned children, and the breakdown of the extended family. Others point out, however, that these trends have had less to do with Iraqis and more to do with the overall shape of the local economy. As one former minister stated, "If the people can't eat, the crime rate will go up." Even those who do not attribute negative changes in Jordan to the Iraqis admit that the "quality and quantity" of violent crime has increased with the growth of the Iraqi expatriate community. This perception is backed by statistics.[52]

Perhaps the most conspicuous of Iraqi-related crimes were the "mafia-style" killings in Amman in 1998. On January 17 of that year, six Iraqis and two Egyptians were stabbed to death in a villa in the exclusive Amman neighborhood of al-Rabiyeh. Those killed included three Iraqi businessmen—millionaire Sami George, Namir Uji, and Iraqi Kurd Numayr Shakir, who operated between Beirut, Amman, and Baghdad—as well as Iraqi diplomat Hikmat Haju, who was then serving as deputy chief of mission at Iraq's embassy in Amman.

Although Jordan's interior minister commented three days after the massacre that "the crime has no political motives," other reports suggested that the perpetrators "spoke with an Iraqi accent."[53] In March 1999, the Jordanian State Security Court convicted and sentenced Muhammed Jaghameen and Ahmad Muhammed Subeh (in absentia) to death for their roles in the crime. Two other individuals were sentenced to twenty years of hard labor. The Jordanian Court of Cassation ratified the death sentences in February 2000.

While the circumstances remain unclear, the fact that Jaghameen was said to be a member of the Iraqi-directed Arab Liberation Front, has led many to speculate that the killings were somehow related to the defection of Hussein Kamel. (Two years earlier, Kamel fled Iraq, allegedly with nearly $1 billion of Saddam's cash.) Yet another rumored explanation for the killings was Namir Uji's ties to Saddam. Uji was said to have run an Amman-based front company for Saddam specializing in Oil-for-Food trade and illegal arms shipments. He allegedly owed millions of dollars to the Iraqi ruling clique.

IRAQI SUPPORT FOR THE JORDANIAN
OPPOSITION TO THE REGIME

The Arab Socialist Ba'th Party in Jordan—which took an active role in the 1996 bread riots—is widely believed to have close ties to Iraq. In addition, Saddam has, over the years, developed a strong base of support in the Kingdom among Islamists and Palestinians. These connections, more than the small, ineffectual, and closely monitored Jordanian Ba'th party, comprise some of Saddam's best inroads into the Kingdom.

Islamists in Jordan have been a generally loyal but at times problematic element of opposition to the Hashemites. During the 1996 and 1998 bread riots, the Muslim Brotherhood and its political party, the IAF, were quick to state their fealty to the king. At other times, however, IAF complaints and criticisms of the Jordanian monarch seemed designed to undermine key elements of regime support and legitimacy. Usually, these complaints focused on the Kingdom's ties to Israel and the United States, as well as Jordan's nominal adherence to the sanctions against Iraq. Long-standing IAF strategies for mobilizing popular support have in the past proved an embarrassment to the monarchy. Moreover, they highlight the strong subterranean support for Saddam in the Kingdom.

A leading Islamist advocate for Saddam in Jordan is Laith Shubeilat, former head of the Engineer's Association. Son of a former pro-British defense minister, Shubeilat is a controversial but respected figure in the Kingdom. He was once imprisoned and later pardoned by King Hussein for his alleged involvement in a militant Islamic plot to topple the monarchy. It is also said that Shubeilat receives funding directly from Saddam. More than financial assistance, however, Shubeilat, who routinely visits Iraq, has in recent years been the recipient of excellent public relations and media coverage in Jordan courtesy of Baghdad. Most famously, in January 1998, Shubeilat single-handedly secured the release of ninety-two Jordanian prisoners being held in Iraq. The Shubeilat-brokered release, announced just after his meeting with Saddam in Baghdad, was an acute embarrassment for the Jordanian government. Coming just months after the execution of four Jordanians in Iraq (who were accused of smuggling automobile spare parts), it appears that the prisoner release was a move calculated to build good public relations for Saddam among Jordanians. In the process, Saddam enhanced the domestic appeal and stature of Shubeilat, the regime's long-time Islamist nemesis. On his return to Jordan, Shubeilat was taken into custody but was soon released.

In February 1998—a month after he returned from Baghdad—Shubeilat once again made headlines in connection with Iraq. That month, as the United States was gearing up for a military strike against Iraq, Shubeilat accused the Jordanian government of participating in "the conspiracy against our brothers in Iraq."[54] Later that month, Shubeilat was arrested for his role in fomenting a pro-Iraqi demonstration in Ma'an. In the aftermath of his arrest, Shubeilat condemned the government—and, perhaps by extension, the king—as "Zionist and hostile to Iraq."[55]

Of course, Shubeilat is not the only Jordanian Islamist with ongoing ties to the regime in Baghdad. Iraqi leaders routinely meet with the top leadership of the IAF. In 1997, Tariq Aziz met with then IAF secretary general Muhammad

Uwaydah. In addition, Hamza Mansour, a leading IAF activist, is a regular visitor to Baghdad.

Like his relationship with the Jordanian Islamists, Saddam's relationship with the Palestinians provides Iraq with significant influence in the Kingdom. With a Jordanian population believed to be at least 60 percent Palestinian, Iraq's position on the Israeli–Palestianian conflict curries a lot of favor.

Historically, of course, this was not always the case. It is said that in 1968–1970, Jordanian prime minister Wasfi al-Tel convinced the Iraqis that Palestinian factions should not take over Jordan.[56] Hence, when the Palestine Liberation Organization (PLO) under Chairman Yasser Arafat tried to take over the Kingdom in 1970, Baghdad did not place its twenty-five thousand troops stationed in Jordan under PLO command, as Iraq had previously suggested it would do. Indeed, in the late 1980s, Saddam specifically called on the PLO to respect Jordan's sovereignty.[57]

Iraq's apparent efforts to help maintain Jordanian stability in the 1980s were logical. At the time, Iraq was at war with Iran, and the Kingdom served as the main point of entry to Iraq. Saddam's "hands-off Jordan" orders to the PLO were not at all indicative of a strain in the long-standing relationship between Arafat and Saddam. Indeed, it is said that many PLO fighters were hosted in Iraq following their expulsion from Lebanon in 1982. And some suggest that Arafat actually assisted Saddam—via the thousands of Palestinian expatriate workers in the Kuwaiti financial sector—to dismantle and pilfer Kuwaiti bank accounts.

By the time Iraq invaded Kuwait in 1991, Arafat was a marginalized figure. The Palestinian intifada, the uprising launched against Israel in 1987, was an indigenous affair over which the PLO had little control. And one of Arafat's few remaining allies in the Arab world was Saddam Hussein. The launching of Iraqi SCUD missiles toward Israel during the war confirmed Saddam's (and Iraq's) support for the Palestinian cause and cemented the loyalty of Palestinians in the West Bank and Gaza as well as in Jordan.

While an armed Palestinian insurrection similar to the one that took place in 1970 is not currently a concern in Jordan, Palestinians still possess the ability to destabilize the Kingdom. Saddam's ties to Arafat—as well as Saddam's popularity among many segments of Jordanian society—could be used to trigger mischief in Amman. Saddam could, for example, attempt to manipulate Jordan's economy via the Palestinians. According to most estimates, more than 400 million Jordanian Dinars (JD) are held by West Bank Palestinians, who could—with the proper encouragement—trigger a currency crisis by exchanging those JD en masse for dollars.[58] This potential for volatility was illustrated by the sudden 10 percent drop in the dinar's value in February 1999, when Palestinians sold dinars at the news of King Hussein's death.

Moreover, there is little indication that Yasser Arafat has changed his stripes regarding his longtime territorial designs in Jordan. Shortly after King Abdullah came to power in November 1999, Arafat floated the trial balloon of "confederation" to see how the new monarch would handle this rhetorical challenge. The king deflected the topic, but there are signs that he remains wary of, and alert to, PLO attempts to manipulate Jordanian affairs. For example, in 1999 and 2000, the Kingdom denied entry to some top-ranking PLO officials, including Hani al-Hassan and Abbas Zaki.[59] It is likely that this policy decision was based on the belief that the officials would create problems for the king in the Palestinian refugee camps. The longtime distrust of Arafat's intentions is also reflected in the fact that Palestinian newspapers were not allowed to be sold in Jordan until 1999, ending a ban first put into place following the 1967 war. Likewise, the long-standing Jordanian mistrust is reflected by Jordanian signals in January 2001 that top officials in the Kingdom would prefer Israel to remain in the Jordan Valley (rather than have Israel cede the region to an Arafat-led Palestine) in the event of an Israeli–Palestinian peace settlement.[60]

During the past decade, Iraq and the Palestinians have played key roles in some of the Kingdom's most dangerous moments, especially when the survival of Jordan as a Hashemite realm has been in question: the 1991 Gulf War, the bread riots of 1996, the pro-Iraq riots of 1998, and, most recently, the second Palestinian intifada, initiated in September 2000.

INSTIGATION OF RIOTS?

Rami Khoury, a prominent Jordanian commentator, referred to the 1996 violence in southern Jordan when he wrote: "External hands are nothing new for Jordan. What is new is that in recent years we have suffered domestic disappointments and discontent that provide the environment in which external parties can try to do their dirty deeds."[61] As previously discussed, in conjunction with a series of International Monetary Fund–mandated reforms, the Jordanian government removed all bread subsidies in August 1996. As a result, the price of bread in the Kingdom more than doubled overnight. In the days after the subsidy ended, Jordan—particularly, several of the poorer areas in the south, notably Kerak—was rocked by three days of rioting in protest of the new policy.

The bread riots, as they came to be known, came as a shock. Rather than blame the policy change for the violence, however, top officials in Jordan almost uniformly held Iraq responsible. King Hussein blamed the clashes on "foreign circles." The rioters, he said, "were either educated in Iraq or had sympathies toward Iraq." Then prime minister Kabariti likewise fingered the pro-Iraq Jordanian Ba'th party for fomenting the riots. Several members of the party were arrested during the violence in Kerak.

To date, Baghdad's role in the riots remains unclear. While there was clearly a high level of frustration in the Kingdom in 1996—over the lack of a "peace dividend" with Israel, the continued high unemployment rate, and the ongoing UN boycott of Iraq—there was no definitive "smoking gun" tying the riots to Iraq.

Some analysts suggest that Saddam triggered the riots to engineer Kabariti's removal. He had been the leading proponent of an immediate (as opposed to gradual) removal of the subsidies.[62] Iraq had made no secret of its displeasure with Kabariti, and in the aftermath of the riots, he was in fact sacked.

This explanation seems plausible but highly speculative. A more likely explanation for Iraqi complicity in the rioting was that it served as a message from Saddam to King Hussein that Jordan should stay out of Iraqi internal affairs. Just prior to the problems in Kerak, Jordan itself was implicated in a failed INA coup attempt in Baghdad.

In the absence of definitive proof implicating Baghdad in the bread riots, the most conservative explanation would seem to be that the violence was fueled by pro-Iraqi individuals and political parties, with only limited, if any, official Iraqi involvement.

Interestingly, one of the few Jordanian officials at the time to publicly exonerate Baghdad from responsibility for the riots was then minister of trade and industry Ali Abu Ragheb.[63] In June 2000, the same Abu Ragheb was named by King Abdullah as prime minister, and he immediately embarked on a campaign to repair Jordanian–Iraqi economic relations.

CONTINUED IRAQI MEDDLING

Since Abu Ragheb's appointment, there have been frequent hints that a return to the heyday of Jordanian–Iraqi relations would be in the offing. But for a number of reasons, a full rapprochement has not come to fruition. Perhaps the spillover of the Palestinian uprising, which at times has taken the form of pro-Saddam rallies inside Jordan, has affected the king's thinking. Surely, one of the most important factors has been Jordanian apprehension that the United States would not look kindly upon a warming of Baghdad–Amman ties.

The competing pulls of Iraq and the United States were especially acute in 2001. At the same time that a U.S.–Jordan Free Trade Agreement (FTA) was pending before the U.S. Congress, Amman was weighing the potential benefits of a separate free trade accord with Iraq, which Saddam had offered the Kingdom some months earlier. The Amman business community was clamoring for the king to sign the Iraqi deal; after all, pro-U.S. Egypt had already signed its own FTA with Baghdad. No doubt, Jordanian officials were concerned with how an FTA with Iraq would go over in the United States, and particularly how it would affect the Kingdom's standing with Congress.[64]

Jordanian officials vigorously denied that Washington had exerted pressure on Amman not to sign a deal with Iraq.[65] But clearly Jordan was sensing some type of pressure, given that Jordan's ambassador to the United States Marwan Muasher felt compelled in February 2001 to circulate a "Dear Friend" letter to U.S. officials explaining his government's position on an Iraq FTA.[66]

By delaying a formal decision on the Iraq front, King Abdullah was in fact signaling that the agreement with the United States was the Jordanian priority. Not surprisingly, this assessment provoked Saddam's ire. On March 26—two days prior to the convening of the Arab Summit in Amman—Iraqi vice president Taha Yassin Ramadan publicly lambasted Jordan for its pro-West, pro-Israel positions.[67] During his ninety-minute lecture to a Jordanian delegation in Baghdad, Ramadan roundly condemned Jordan for arresting members of the Anti-Normalization Committee. He also accused King Abdullah of allowing "Jews and Americans" to enter Jordan to "spy" on Iraq.

Perhaps more damaging than these criticisms, however, were Ramadan's allegations that Jordan did not want an FTA with Iraq. "I doubt they are serious," he stated. Then he added, "The brothers in the Jordanian government have backed down on implementing the July trade protocol." Unlike Jordan, he suggested, Baghdad was not interested in an agreement just for "media consumption." As evidence of Jordan's callous disregard for Iraq, Ramadan pointed to Aqaba and the Jordanian pressure for greater Iraqi utilization of the port. "How will I import only through Aqaba?" he asked. "In Aqaba, our goods are thrown in warehouses and sometimes get rotten." Ramadan also implicitly criticized Amman's ongoing participation in the UN inspections regime. The Iraqi vice president ended his tirade with a call on patriotic Jordanians to topple their government, demanding that the "Arab Street should act to put pressure to achieve the objectives of the people, not the objectives of the regime."

Lest this incident be viewed as an aberration, a similar theme was picked up two days later when another Iraqi vice president, Izzat Ibrahim, addressed the Arab Summit and, before a stunned King Abdullah, delivered a speech in Saddam's name that praised the 1958 revolution against the Hashemites in Iraq in which many of the king's uncles and cousins were slaughtered by rebels.[68] Indeed, Saddam cited the revolution as evidence of Iraq's "faith and Arabism." In addition to blatantly insulting King Abdullah and the Hashemites, the speech was an explicit Iraqi condemnation of the Jordanian regime.

CONCLUSION

Iraqi influence pervades Jordan. There is a strong base of support for Iraq among the elite business community in Amman and a vocal network of popular support among a loose coalition of anti-Israel, anti-West Islamists.

Moreover, thousands of Jordanians have attended university in Baghdad, and up to four hundred thousand Iraqis—some of whom are undoubtedly agents of Saddam—reside in the Kingdom. Despite the best efforts of King Abdullah and King Hussein before him—both of whom recognized the inherent danger of this situation—little has been done to counter the Iraqi sway. Jordan today is as vulnerable (if not more so) to Iraqi meddling as it was in the early 1990s. If he so chose, there is little doubt that Saddam could destabilize the Hashemite regime in Amman.

NOTES

1. Jane Mayer and Geraldine Brooks, "How Saddam Hussein Courted Mideast Press with Cars and Cash," *Wall Street Journal*, February 15, 1991, sec A.

2. "Prospects for Renewed Russian-Iraqi Relations Discussed," *Moskovskiye Novosti*, May 1–8, 1994, cited in FBIS-USR-94-057, June 2, 1994. This report is based on information published in April 1994 in *Al-Watan al-Arabi*.

3. Salameh Ne'emat, "Mukhawif Urduniyya min ikhtiraq Iraqi," *Al-Hayat*, September 20, 1995.

4. Salameh Ne'matt, interview by author, detailed notes, Amman, Jordan, September 30, 1999. This was corroborated by another Amman-based journalist.

5. Martin Seiff, "Jordan's King Seeks U.S.–Iraq Dialogue: But Washington Has Dismissed the Idea," *Washington Times*, March 20, 1998. In 2000 Masarweh wrote against the privatization of the Jordanian press and in support of continued Jordanian government "control" of the media. See Tariq Masarweh, "Sahafa al-watan, sahafa al-nitham," *Al-Ra'i*, June 28, 2000.

6. Fahd al-Fanik, "Columnist Says Lloyd's Inspections 'Obvious Humiliation,' " *Jordan Times*, February 23, 1997, cited in Federal Broadcast Information Service-Near East and South Asia (FBIS-NES-97-036), February 25, 1997.

7. Fahd al-Fanik, "PM's Visit to Iraq Gave Dividends," *Jordan Times*, November 13, 2000.

8. Hani al-Khasawneh, interview by author, detailed notes, Amman, Jordan, October 5, 1999.

9. Iyad al-Tubasi, "Hani al-Khasawneh: hisar al-Iraq yati duman al-mu'amara al-sihuyniyya ala al-Umma," *Al-Sabil*, October 5, 1999.

10. Hani al-Khasawneh, interview by author, detailed notes, Amman, Jordan, October 5, 1999.

11. "Hani al-Khasawneh: Wazir Urduni wa Ba'athi sabiq, namuthij izdiwajiyya al-khtab al-siyasi al-Urduni al-mu'arid," *Al-Malaf al-Iraqi*, February 1996, reprinted from *Al-Aswaq*, January 20, 1996.

12. Ahmed al-Shuruf, "Jordan Bar Association Wants to Hire Private Plane to Fly Bar Association Members," *Al-Dustur*, February 25, 2000, cited in FBIS-NES-2000-0229, March 1, 2000.

13. Ahmed Abd al-Majid, "Baghdad to Hold 'Biggest' Unionists Rally 27 February," *Al-Dustur*, February 24, 1999, cited in FBIS-NES-1999-0228, February 27, 1999.

14. Ahmed al-Sharuf, "Idan al-adwan al-Amriki al-Britani did al-Iraq watalab bi-rafa al-hisar," *Al-Dustur*, March 1, 1999.

15. "Third Day of Anti-U.S. Protests in Jordan," Agence France Presse, December 19, 1998.

16. "Our Profile," Amman Chamber of Industry website, www.aci.org.jo, 2002 [accessed February 13, 2003].

17. Khaldoun Abu Hassan, interview by author, detailed notes, Amman, Jordan, October 12, 1999.

18. "Nashatat ghurfat al-sina'at Amman nahu ta'ziz al-ilaqat al-iqtisadiyyah al-Urduniyya al-Iraqiyya," undated publication of the Amman Chamber of Industry.

19. Khaldoun Abu Hassan, interview by author, detailed notes, Amman, Jordan, October 12, 1999.

20. Khaldoun Abu Hassan, interview by author, detailed notes, Amman, Jordan, October 12, 1999.

21. "Trade Delegation Leaves for Talks in Baghdad," *Jordan Times*, September 11, 1999, cited in FBIS-NES-1999-0911, September 13, 1999.

22. On February 15, 1998, for example, Iraqi minister of trade Muhammad Mahdi Saleh gave a talk for the Chamber at the ACI offices in Amman. "Nashatat ghurfat al-sina'at Amman nahu ta'ziz al-ilaqat al-iqtisadiyyah al-Urduniyya al-Iraqiyya," undated publication of the Amman Chamber of Industry.

23. Bassam Badreen, "Qalaq Iraqi tijah al-tajawab al-Urduni maa Amrika fi harbha did asalib al-tahayil ala al-hisar'," *Al-Quds al-Arabi*, May 19, 2000.

24. Salama al-Dirawi, "Sina'yu Amman yantakhibun majlis idarat al-ghurfat al-yawm," *Arab al-Yawm*, May 11, 2000.

25. "Amman: 58 Alf nashit siyasi wa naqabi yutalibun bimubadara arabiyya litafkik al-hathr ala al-Iraq," *Al-Quds al-Arabi*, May 17, 2000.

26. See, for example, "Ghurfat al-tijarat Amman tatabara milyun qalam rasas lil-Iraq," *Al-Dustur*, February 8, 2000.

27. "Basic Figures," www.un.org/depts/oip, October 29, 2002 [accessed February 13, 2002].

28. "Tariq Aziz Addresses Jordanian Delegation," Baghdad Iraq Television, February 4, 2000, cited in FBIS-NES-2000-0205, February 7, 2000. The speech was recorded on February 2, 2000.

29. "Pencil Convoy Leader on U.S. Attempt to 'Obstruct' Mission," Baghdad Iraq Television, January 31, 2000, cited in FBIS-NES-2000-0131, February 1, 2000.

30. Atif al-Julani, "Ziyara fil waqt al-sahih," *Al-Sabeel*, November 15, 2000.

31. In 1998–1999, according to the Kingdom's Council of Higher Education statistics section, a total of 21,408 Jordanian students studied abroad. Of these, 3,234 students were in Syria, 2,984 in Iraq, and 2,629 in Lebanon. *Al-Ihsaa'i al-taliba al-Urduniyyin fi mu'asasat al-ta'alim al-aliya kharig al-Urdun li'aam 1998–1999,* Jordan Council of Higher Education, General Secretariat, 17. By way of comparison, only 1,922 Jordanian students studied in the United States, almost half of whom were in graduate programs.

32. "Al-taqrir al-ihsaa'i al-sanawi an al-ta'alim al-ali fil Urdun li'aam 1997–1998," Jordan Council of Higher Education, General Secretariat, 86.

33. "Al-taqrir al-ihsaa'i al-sanawi an al-ta'alim al-ali fil Urdun li'aam 1997–1998," Jordan Council of Higher Education, General Secretariat, 98.

34. *Jordanian Students Renew "Pledge" to Saddam*, Baghdad Iraq Television Network, September 3, 1995, cited in FBIS-NES-95-172, September 6, 1995.

35. "Murasil '*Al-Hayat*' fil-Urdun sijun bisabab khab 'Al-Ikhtiraq al-Iraqi,'" *Al-Hayat*, October 4, 1996.

36. Muhammed al-Najar, "Man hu al-mustafid min takhrib ilaqat al-Urdun wal-Iraq?" *Al-Sabil*, February 15–21, 2000.

37. Muhammed al-Najar, "Man hu al-mustafid min takhrib ilaqat al-Urdun wal-Iraq?" *Al-Sabil*, February 15–21, 2000.

38. "Prime Minister Describes Iraq as a 'Big Prison,'" *Jordan Times*, April 2, 1996, cited in FBIS-NES-96-065, April 4, 1996.

39. "Sahafa Urduniyya: Baghdad tarfud al-ta'amul maa huwkumat al-Kabariti," *Al-Malaf al-Iraqi*, February 1997. *Al-Malaf al-Iraqi* cited in an article from *Al-Quds al-Arabi* on January 11, 1997.

40. Nahid Hattar, "Jordanian Islamist Shubaylat on New King Abdullah," *Al-Safir*, March 18, 1999, cited in FBIS-NES-1999-032, April 23, 1999.

41. Muhammed al-Najar, "Man hu al-mustafid min takhrib ilaqat al-Urdun wal-Iraq?" *Al-Sabil*, February 15–21, 2000.

42. "Al-Kabariti on Achievements, Regional Ties," *Al-Majallah*, March 9–15, 1997, cited in FBIS-NES-97-048, March 14, 1997.

43. "Iraqi Opposition Official's Brother Commits Suicide in Amman," Agence France Presse, November 30, 1998.

44. Con Coghlin, "Saddam Told Me to Kill Dissident in London," *Sunday Telegraph (London)*, August 22, 1999.

45. "Jordanian Minister on Opposition, Iraq," *Al-Majallah*, March 22–28, 1998, cited in FBIS-NES-98-085, March 27, 1998.

46. Eid al-Fayez, interview by author, detailed notes, Amman, Jordan, October 2, 1999.

47. Muhammed Asfour, interview by author, detailed notes, Amman, Jordan, June 29, 2000.

48. Yanal al-Bustami, interview by author, detailed notes, Amman, Jordan, October 2, 1999.

49. Salameh Ne'matt, "Al-Urdun yatakhith ijra'at qad tua'di ila tarad ma'at al-alaf al-amal al-wafidin," *Al-Hayat*, October 6, 1998.

50. Talib al-Ahmed, "Al-Iraqiyun fil-Urdun: Nahnu huna . . . Inqathuna?" *Al-Dusturiyya*, no. 6 (May 1996).

51. Lola Keilani, "Ph.D. Holders for Hire," *Al-Ahram Weekly*, no. 499 (September 14–20, 2001).

52. "Crime Increases in Jordan," Middle East News Line, January 12, 2000.

53. "Jordan, Iraq Agree on Killers' Aims, Disagree on Probe," *Al-Sharq al-Awsat*, January 20, 1998, cited in FBIS-NES-98-020, January 21, 1998.

54. Tariq Ayyoub, "Jordan Opposition Denounces U.S. Military Action against Iraq," *Jordan Times*, February 10, 1998, cited in FBIS-NES-98-041, February 10, 1998.

55. Tariq Ayyoub, "Iraqi Figures Protest Arrest of Shubeilat," *Jordan Times*, March 5, 1998, cited in FBIS-NES-98-060, March 5, 1998.

56. Jamal al-Sha'ir, interview by author, detailed notes, Amman, Jordan, July 8, 2000.

57. Amatzia Baram, "Ba'athi Iraq and Hashemite Jordan: From Hostility to Alignment," *Middle East Journal* 45, no. 1 (winter 1991).

58. Munir Soubir, interview by author, detailed notes, Amman, Jordan, October 4, 2000.

59. "Jordan Bans Fatah Members from Visiting Camps," *Al-Sharq al-Awsat*, January 6, 2001, cited in FBIS-NES-2000-0106, January 7, 2001.

60. Ze'ev Schiff, "Jordan Wants Israel to Stay in Jordan Valley," *Ha'aretz*, January 12, 2001. Other Jordanian security officials confirmed this assessment off-the-record.

61. "Jordan Arrests Opposition Activists, but Charge of Iraqi Responsibility Doesn't Wash," *Mideast Mirror*, August 20, 1996.

62. Kabariti differed from much of the Jordanian leadership in this regard. Prince Hassan, for example, had advocated a gradual removal of subsidies, which, he argued, would be more conducive in the short term to the Kingdom's stability.

63. Natasha al-Bukhari, "Officials Say Ties with Iraq Not to Suffer Due to Riots," *Jordan Times*, August 21, 1996, cited in FBIS-NES-96-163, August 23, 1996.

64. "Al-Urdun: yataraqab rad al-fa'il al-Amriki ala itifaqiyyat at-tijara al-hura maa al-Iraq," *Al-Quds al-Arabi*, April 5, 2001.

65. See, for example, Information Minister Taleb Rifai in Rana Awwad, "No U.S. Pressure on Jordan Not to Sign FTA with Iraq-Jordan," *Jordan Times*, February 15, 2001.

66. See appendix C for the text of the February 5 letter.

67. "Taha Ramadan: al-Saudiyya tumawil al-gharat al-Amrikiyya did al-Iraq," *Al-Quds al-Arabi*, March 26, 2001.

68. "President Saddam Hussein's Address to the Arab Summit Amman," Iraq News Agency, March 27, 2001.

Chapter Four

The Abdullah Era

A NEW TACK

The death of King Hussein in 1999 marked the end of an era in Jordan. King Hussein had ruled for nearly five decades, shaping Jordan's foreign and domestic policy seemingly by force of personality. He was the only ruler most Jordanians had ever known. Adding to the shock, King Hussein was replaced not by his brother Prince Hassan—who had served as crown prince since 1965—but by Abdullah, his eldest son. This abrupt change of plan occurred only days before King Hussein's death.

While Jordanians were familiar with Hassan, the newly anointed Abdullah was a relative unknown. Long part of the Jordanian military establishment—since 1994 he had served as commander of the Special Forces and later of the Special Operations Command—Abdullah did not maintain a particularly high profile in the royal family. But despite his relative obscurity, many in Amman and Washington, were optimistic about the change. Abdullah was, so the thinking went, part of a "new generation" of Middle Eastern leaders, more at ease with the West and the modern world. His mother was British, he attended prep school and college in the United States, and his facility in English was better than in Arabic. Given this background, it was widely assumed that Abdullah would have a moderate, pro-West political orientation.

So far, in the early years of his reign, it is clear that King Abdullah has made improving relations with the United States a high priority. At the same time, he has worked—and largely succeeded—to repair Jordan's strained ties with Baghdad. In a sense, Abdullah's initial years in power suggest a degree of continuity from his father's reign. Indeed, the balancing act between Baghdad and Washington has been a hallmark of Jordanian foreign policy since 1990, with Jordan's strategic orientation sometimes leaning toward its leading trade partner, Iraq, and at other times toward its regional security patron, the United States.

Continuity, however, does not mean that Abdullah's approach is identical to Hussein's. Instead of alternating between these two important bilateral relationships, Abdullah seems to be trying to improve ties with both simultaneously. Whether Jordan can maintain this high-wire act for long is uncertain, especially as U.S.–Iraq war clouds begin to gather. And the fate of the policy will have profound implications for the security and stability of the Hashemite regime in Jordan.

FIRST STEPS

At the end of the traditional Muslim forty-day mourning period, King Abdullah undertook a series of state visits, during which he met with various Arab leaders and requested debt forgiveness and economic assistance for Jordan. The new king made no secret of his focus on improving the Kingdom's economy. At the same time, Abdullah started making overtures to Iraq, signaling his inclination toward repairing ties with Baghdad. In April 1999 just prior to his departure for one of his first state visits, Abdullah spelled out the revamped policy. "We in Jordan are in the start of a new era where we are giving priority to our internal situation," he said, adding, "We [Jordanians] have no aspirations for any regional role in Iraq or other countries."[1] His statement was clarified in the official daily *al-Dustur* as meaning there would be no Jordanian "military or political intervention" in Iraq.

Although Abdullah was making conciliatory statements toward Baghdad, the appointment of his first government in March 1999 provided little indication of his intentions. Abdullah's new prime minister, Abdul Rawouf Rawabdeh, was a veteran politician from northern Jordan with ties to the Muslim Brotherhood; Rawabdeh was generally thought to have pro-Iraq sympathies, but he was not commonly identified as a leader of the "Iraq lobby." Abdullah's choice for chief of the Royal Court, however, was Abdel Karim al-Kabariti, well known for his close ties to Saudi Arabia and Kuwait—indeed, he was the chairman of the Jordan–Kuwait Bank—and a longtime, outspoken critic of Saddam.

In his letter appointing the new cabinet, however, King Abdullah did give some clue as to how the Kingdom would proceed with regard to Iraq. He urged "continued dialogue with all Arab states without exception" while at the same time continuing Jordan's efforts to end the "suffering and embargo" on the Iraqi people. This approach was confirmed during Abduallah's inaugural visit to Washington as king in May 1999. Asked about Iraq by Peter Jennings of ABC News, Abdullah openly acknowledged that he would "like the sanctions lifted."[2] When pressed by Jennings about whether the removal of Saddam was a prerequisite for the reintegration of Iraq into the region, Abdullah reiterated the new Jordanian policy of nonintervention. "That is something," he said, "that is left up to Saddam and the Iraqi people."

King Abdullah was urging an immediate end to sanctions, but unlike before, these statements were no longer coupled with the stipulation that Iraq comply with all relevant UN resolutions. Jordan's new position was clearly articulated in a May 12, 1999, interview with the London independent Arabic daily *al-Hayat*, in which the king simply stated: "We look forward to change that saves the Iraqi people from their current ordeal."[3]

In August—in a move some speculated would annoy Iraq—Jordan reopened its embassy in Kuwait, signaling the end of the decade of estrangement between these two states. King Abdullah and his wife, Queen Rania, a Palestinian born in Kuwait, visited Kuwait City in early September. Interestingly, at about the same time that King Abdullah was patching up ties with pro-U.S. Kuwait, reports surfaced suggesting that the long-dormant Iraqi opposition was no longer welcome in Jordan.[4]

After a round of visits in Europe and the Middle East, King Abdullah prepared for his second state visit to the United States in October. Just prior to his departure, media reports centered on the king's possible role as a mediator between Baghdad and Washington. Of course, this would not have been unusual, given that his father had frequently played such a role. According to reports, Iraqi prime minister Tariq Aziz passed a letter to his Jordanian counterpart in early October conveying an Iraqi request for Abdullah to make "efforts to secure an acceptable formula for relations between Iraq and the United States."[5] Several press reports of questionable veracity reported the actual contents of the letter. While Abdullah himself confirmed that Aziz had indeed "passed a message" intended for President Bill Clinton, he declined to comment on its contents. Acknowledging the letter, Kabariti insisted that the king would "certainly not plead the Iraqi case."[6]

King Abdullah met with Clinton on October 12, but according to State Department officials, he did not deliver the alleged Iraqi message. It appears that King Abdullah avoided public discussion of Iraq during the visit, instead focusing solely on his economic requests. Nevertheless, he maintained his strong advocacy on behalf of terminating UN sanctions on Iraq. In early November, back in Amman, Abdullah delivered a speech to the Jordanian parliament calling on the international community to "fulfill its human and moral duty" to lift the sanctions. Near the end of his first year as king, Abdullah summarized the "strategic" rationale underlying the Jordanian position on Iraq: "We have repeatedly expressed apprehension that the tragic situation in Iraq could result in the partition of that country, and this would be a catastrophe because safeguarding the integrity of Iraq is in everyone's interest."[7]

The first major breakthrough for Jordanian–Iraqi relations in the Abdullah era came in December 1999, when the annual oil protocol negotiations stalled. As with some previous years, these negotiations—which essentially determine the extent of Iraq's annual oil subsidy to Jordan—were quite contentious. This year, however, the discussions were more rancorous than usual, and in order to break the deadlock, King Abdullah dispatched Jordanian foreign minister Abdul Ilah al-Khatib to Iraq for discussions with Iraqi deputy prime minister Tariq Aziz on December 22. Khatib's visit constituted the first visit of an Arab foreign minister to Iraq since the 1991 Gulf War.

Two weeks later, on January 15, Kabariti, who had for several weeks been rumored to be on his way out, resigned his position as chief of the Royal Court and was replaced by former prime minister and Jordan–Israel peace negotiator Fayez Tarawneh. Not coincidentally, it was reported about this time that Amman had acceded to the long-standing request from Baghdad that the Kingdom restrict the activities of the Iraqi opposition in Amman.[8] Talks between the two states resumed, and a few days later the annual oil protocol—widely considered to be the most favorable deal for Jordan ever negotiated—was signed.

On April 3, two months after the protocol was completed, Iraq once again became the center of attention for Jordan when an Italian-registered plane piloted by an Italian national named Nicola Trivoni flew from Amman via Syrian airspace to Baghdad on a "humanitarian mission." Trivoni's flight, intended to shine a press spotlight on the suffering of the Iraqi people under sanctions, placed the Jordanian government in an awkward position. After all, Jordan consistently called for the lifting of sanctions but was, nominally at least, adhering to them.

On his return to Jordan, Trivoni was arrested and his plane impounded, but in a matter of days, he became an icon in Jordan. Saleh Armouti, head of the pro-Iraq, Islamist-controlled Lawyer's Union, met with Trivoni in prison and announced that the union would provide Trivoni with pro bono legal counsel. The union also agreed to cover all Trivoni's expenses in Jordan. Trivoni was allowed to leave Jordan on April 9, but he was later found guilty in absentia and sentenced to three years in prison for violating Jordan's airspace and "exposing Jordanian aviation to danger." In response, the speaker of Iraq's parliament sent a letter to Jordan's lower house asking them to intervene and cancel the sentence.

Several days after Trivoni's arrest, the London-based *al-Quds al-Arabi* described him as a "popular hero."[9] It is easy to see why, as Trivoni's arrest proved the catalyst for a wave of pro-Iraq sentiment in Jordan, highlighted by a petition from parliament to the king that he authorize Jordanian flights into Iraq. This petition would form the basis of the Jordanian decision to resume flights into Baghdad some months later.

To some degree, it appears that the mass support for Trivoni's escapade was heightened by the coincidental visit of U.S. secretary of defense William Cohen to Jordan on April 4. When asked about the Italian pilot during a press conference that day, Cohen credited the king "and the Jordanian people [who] understand that Saddam Hussein continues to pose a threat to the region."[10] He also blamed Saddam for "deliberately inflicting harm on his own people" in order to make their plight more telegenic and stir up international efforts to end UN sanctions. That Cohen made this case in Amman at the moment when most Jordanians were hailing Trivoni as a hero only highlighted the gap between popular opinion in Jordan and the United States. Apparently, the Jordanian government also found Cohen's comments problematic, prompting Minister of Information Saleh al-Qalab to issue a statement the next day distancing the government from Cohen.[11] Qalab said, "Jordan respects the will of the Iraqi people and its choice" of Saddam. Moreover, he added, everything that Cohen said during the press conference "reflects his [own] country's position" and not that of Jordan.

By May 2000, Abdullah's Iraq policy had crystallized. During a meeting with U.S. assistant secretary of state for Near Eastern affairs Martin Indyk, he stated that Jordan's position on Iraq "was based on the Arab stand calling for the lifting of sanctions on the Iraqi people" and reiterated that Jordan "would not be party to initiating any change whatsoever in Iraq." The king added that sanctions had become a "great moral disgrace."[12] This meeting set the stage for Jordan's summer 2000 rapprochement with Iraq.

KING ABDULLAH'S RAPPROCHEMENT WITH IRAQ

Events in June provided little indication that Jordan and Iraq were heading toward a genuine political rapprochement. Indeed, several signals were contradictory. In early June, more than half the members of the Jordanian parliament signed a petition urging the government to lift a ban on civilian flights to Iraq. (One month earlier, the Jordanian government had announced plans to establish a committee to study Iraq's request.)[13] At about the same time, King Abdullah traveled to the United States, where he appeared on CNN's *Larry King Live* and once again called for the lifting of sanctions. When Iraq responded to Abdullah's gracious support by executing a Jordanian national four days later on charges of espionage, Jordanian leaders refused to let the incident mushroom into a crisis. As one official said, "Jordan will not change its stand towards Iraq, we do not think that there will be any tension in the relation" due to the execution.[14] Although one member of the lower house of the Jordanian parliament noted that the execution was probably a "political gesture," suggesting that Iraq was "upset with the Kingdom's policy toward them," he stated that at this point it would probably be better "not to escalate this matter."[15]

On June 6, King Abdullah met with President Clinton for discussions that focused on economic issues and the dominance of Iraq in the Jordanian economy. During this visit Clinton announced the U.S. Free Trade Agreement (FTA) initiative with Jordan. Later that same month, Abdullah also sacked Prime Minister Rawabdeh and replaced him with Ali Abu Ragheb, a former minister of trade and industry and frequent traveler to Baghdad. According to the Amman gossip mill, the Abu Ragheb appointment was designed to signal that King Abdullah was intent on improving relations with Iraq.[16]

THE TAHA YASSIN RAMADAN VISIT

On July 16, 2000, with great fanfare, Iraqi vice president Taha Yassin Ramadan visited Amman for meetings with King Abdullah. Ostensibly, the purpose of Ramadan's trip—the highest ranking Iraqi official to visit Jordan since King Abdullah assumed power in 1999—was to discuss ways to increase bilateral trade and improve overall ties.

For Jordan, the talks came at an opportune time; over the previous six months, Iraqi imports transiting Aqaba had declined significantly. Likewise, the visit of Ramadan provided King Abdullah with the opportunity to rectify some confusion with the Iraqis regarding travel procedures for armed escorts of Iraqi officials who would use Amman as a travel hub, given the ban on air travel via Baghdad. An episode some months earlier at the Jordanian–Iraqi border had triggered a shift wherein the Iraqis opted to use Damascus rather than Amman.

According to reports in the pan-Arab press, Ramadan came bearing gifts for Jordan, but those gifts came at a price. In return for the promise of increased Iraqi utilization of the Aqaba port and a boost in Iraqi imports of Jordanian goods, Ramadan apparently demanded that Jordan promise to end the air embargo on Iraq.[17]

Seemingly, Ramadan's meeting with Jordanian leaders went very well. Reports suggested that a Jordanian trade delegation, possibly led by Prime Minister Abu Ragheb, would soon travel to Baghdad. Abdullah himself confirmed the success of his meetings with Ramadan in a front-page interview with *al-Quds al-Arabi* on July 19, 2000.[18] In that interview, the king stated that a "new page" had been opened in Jordanian–Iraqi relations.

Although real changes in trade policy would take some time to materialize, the early returns for Jordan seemed promising. In early August, the Iraqi ambassador in Jordan assured nervous Jordanians that Baghdad was intent on improving bilateral economic ties, and other reports confirmed that Iraq had indeed already committed to increased utilization of Aqaba.[19] Later that month, Abu Ragheb hosted the Iraqi trade minister and reportedly was told that "Jordan enjoys priority" for Iraqi imports.[20]

Just as Jordanian–Iraqi business contacts were starting to heat up, the issue of the air embargo of Iraq returned to the headlines when a Russian "humanitarian" flight landed in Baghdad in mid-August. The following month, the Russians dispatched another airplane to Baghdad carrying eleven senior Russian oil officials. A similar French flight followed one week later. Both Paris and Moscow maintained that these "humanitarian missions" were in compliance with UN sanctions regulations and stipulated that notification of the Sanctions Committee was the only obligation prior to departure.

Shortly after the first Russian plane touched down at Saddam Airport, a large Jordanian trade delegation headed by Jordanian minister of trade and industry Wasif Azar and minister of transport Mohammed Kaladeh arrived in Baghdad. During these talks, Iraqi vice president Ramadan expressed satisfaction at Jordan's efforts to lift the sanctions. Yet, after the delegation departed, Iraqi rhetoric toward Jordan changed. On September 13, Iraqi minister of trade Muhammad Mahdi Saleh made several statements critical of Jordanian officials—past and present—as well as the quality of Jordanian goods.[21] In addition to broadsides against former Jordanian minister of trade Hani Mulki and Chief of the Royal Court Kabariti, Saleh warned that Iraq would "not continue to accept inferior products from the Jordanian market"— a reference to the often low-quality goods Jordan sold to Iraq during the early years of the sanctions regime when Iraq appeared to be a captive market. In addition, he warned that Iraq would not accept Jordanian normalization with Israel and would continue to implement its secondary boycott of Jordanians doing business with Israel.

Perhaps most significantly, Saleh condemned the meddling of the United States and its ambassador in Amman, William Burns (now U.S. assistant secretary of state), in Jordanian–Iraqi bilateral affairs.[22] The ambassador, Saleh accused, plays a "greater role than it appears" in the Jordanian–Iraqi relationship, a role that he urged Jordan to try to limit. It would be possible, according to Saleh, to solve Jordan's economic problems via cooperation with Iraq, "but the American administration does not want this."

Two weeks after Saleh's comments, a Royal Jordanian Airlines airbus carrying three cabinet members, several members of parliament, a staff of medical workers, and three tons of supplies flew to Baghdad. Like the previous French and Russian flights, Jordan had notified the appropriate UN committee prior to departure. (Jordan's previous request to the UN Sanctions Committee, submitted in February 2000, had been rejected in May.)[23] The Jordanian flight, the first

Arab "embargo-busting" flight in ten years, was widely publicized, and it inaugurated a series of Arab flights to Baghdad, including Egyptian, Syrian, Palestinian, and Yemeni charters. Clearly, Iraq was pleased with Amman's decision to resume the air link with Baghdad. Iraqi vice president Tariq Aziz called for Iraq's friends to "follow the example of Jordan" and dispatch flights to Saddam Airport.[24]

While some commentators speculated that the Jordanian decision to fly to Baghdad was influenced by concerns over a recent warming of Syrian–Iraqi ties—indeed the Royal Jordanian flight beat the Syrian flight only by a matter of days—there was little doubt that Amman would benefit from being the first. In fact, King Abdullah likely calculated that breaking the embargo would be rewarded with a generous oil protocol at the end of the year.

Just to be sure, Abdullah took a few more steps guaranteed to win favor with Saddam. On October 11, just before leaving Amman for Washington for the signing of the first ever FTA between an Arab state and the United States, Abdullah suddenly and unilaterally expelled Lloyd's Register, the agency that had been inspecting all Aqaba shipments transiting to Iraq. Also that month, Jordan agreed to Iraq's demand that all transactions between the two states be carried out in euros as opposed to U.S. dollars.[25] And later that month, at the Cairo Arab Summit, King Abdullah made what serves as his strongest statement to date regarding the sanctions. "Iraq has paid a heavy price," the king said. "Now the time has come to put an end to Iraq's suffering. Our nation is no more able to endure the continued suffering."[26]

Pursuing this pro-Iraq policy, Jordanian prime minister Abu Ragheb traveled to Baghdad in late October 2000 for the first visit of an Arab prime minister to Iraq in ten years. (The last Jordanian prime minister to visit Iraq was Mudar Badran in 1991.) While in Baghdad, Abu Ragheb had an audience with Saddam, but reliable sources describe the dynamic of the meeting as odd. Apparently, Saddam would not let Abu Ragheb discuss the issue of oil. All Saddam evidently talked about was the Palestinian intifada and what Jordan and Iraq could do, separately and together, to support the Palestinians.

When Abu Ragheb returned home, however, he carried a letter to the king from Saddam, thanking Abdullah and the Jordanian people for all they had done to try to end the sanctions.[27] More than any thank-you note, however, the Jordanian–Iraqi oil protocol signed by Abu Ragheb during his stay in Iraq underscored Saddam's pleasure with the status of the bilateral relationship. It was the most propitious agreement for Jordan in years.

In December 2000, figures released by the Jordanian Department of Statistics confirmed the economic benefits to Jordan of the political rapprochement with Iraq. In the first ten months of 2000, the Kingdom's trade with Iraq had increased 60 percent over the same period in 1999.[28] Despite the marked improvement in relations, skeptics like Jordanian journalist Salameh Ne'matt were quick to point out that the Iraqi largesse was not based on altruism or Arab nationalism. Rather, said Ne'matt, "there is an Iraqi political bill" that Jordan must pay. "The terms of this bill have not yet emerged."[29]

THE DUALITY OF IRAQI–JORDANIAN RELATIONS: THE CASE OF LABOR POLICY

Balancing a pro-Iraq and pro-America policy was not an easy task for Jordan. One policy area where there appears to have been a change under King Abdullah concerns the sensitive issue of Iraqi residents in Jordan. Throughout the first year of Abdullah's reign, Jordan's labor ministry pursued a policy that many considered to be Saddam-friendly, but not Iraq-friendly. In July 1999, in an effort to encourage the departure of Iraqis from the Kingdom, the ministry stopped issuing work permits to foreigners—particularly to Iraqis—and mandated the issuing of fines to those contravening labor and residency laws. Essentially, the ministry made it more difficult for Iraqis who did not want to return home to remain in the Kingdom.

Iraqi opposition groups in Amman protested the policy, which they claimed was resulting in deportations and expulsions.[30] Although it is not clear whether this policy intentionally targeted opposition figures, there seemed to be a concerted effort in the late 1990s to thin out the Iraqi population in the Kingdom. Given that top estimates at the time put the Iraqi expatriate population in Jordan at almost 10 percent of the Kingdom's total, it is not surprising that the policy would be geared toward rolling back these numbers. After all, not all Iraqis in Jordan were refugees or oppositionists; many were undoubtedly agents of Saddam. As Labor Minister Eid al-Fayez noted in October 1999, unlike other foreigners, the Iraqis in Jordan pose a definite political problem: "We don't know what they're carrying in their pockets."[31]

In 2000, however, as Jordanian–Iraqi relations improved, it seems that this pro-Saddam labor policy was altered. In November 2000, for example, the Jordanian government decided to exempt Iraqis in violation of labor and residence laws. Under the new policy, Iraqi residents of Jordan would now be excused from paying accumulated fines for overstaying their officially permitted time limits in the Kingdom.[32] Just as Amman was placing restrictions on the activities of the Iraqi opposition, it was making it easier for Iraqis fleeing Saddam to stay in the Kingdom. Such was the nature of the seesaw approach that characterized Jordan–Iraq ties.

IRAQI MOBILIZATION DURING PALESTINIAN "INTIFADA"

In early October 2000, following the start of Palestinian violence, Saddam once again surprised observers, this time by deploying one hundred thousand troops from the Republican Guards' Hammurabi Division west of Baghdad at Rutbah, a junction near the Jordanian border. These units were reinforced in mid-October. Coming on the heels of several large demonstrations in Jordan— where, for the first time in nearly a decade, protestors invoked the name of Saddam[33]—the Iraqi mobilization underscored fears that Saddam might seek to capitalize on his popularity inside the kingdom.

While U.S. officials downplayed this maneuver as a "training" activity, the mobilization was clearly a display of Iraqi support for the Palestinian "intifada" against Israel. It also placed King Abdullah in a potentially precarious position. Early on in the violence, Abdullah had lent vocal support to the Palestinians and had donated some $2 million to the cause. However, the ongoing violence in the West Bank was beginning to spread into the Kingdom. In October alone, there were hundreds of rallies and demonstrations in support of the Palestinians, including one in downtown Amman in which a car with U.S. embassy license plates was attacked.[34] The Jordanian government subsequently banned all demonstrations.

In November, as Israeli–Palestinian clashes reached new heights, Jordanian prime minister Abu Ragheb was dispatched to Baghdad. Though ostensibly geared toward signing the annual oil protocol, this trip was apparently designed to assuage some domestic tension inside Jordan vis-à-vis Amman's support for the Palestinians. Palestinian issues featured prominently on Abu Ragheb's agenda with Iraqi vice president Taha Yassin Ramadan.[35]

In early November, Iraqi units stationed near Rutbah were withdrawn, but the presence of Iraqi troops on Jordan's eastern border had highlighted the risk that Israeli–Palestinian violence could escalate into regional conflict engulfing Jordan. A number of scenarios, though not realized at the time, could have threatened the stability of the regime in Amman. How would King Abdullah have reacted if Saddam requested permission to transit his troops across Jordanian territory to join in the struggle against Israel? Although Jordan is bound by a treaty with Israel to prohibit foreign armies on its soil, the king might not have been able to fend off the domestic pressure to allow Iraqi entry. Thankfully, Saddam never put King Abdullah to the test.

Even after Saddam redeployed his troops from the Jordanian border, he continued to cultivate his ideological supporters in the Palestinian Authority (PA) and in Jordan by providing financial assistance to the families of Palestinian "martyrs" killed in clashes with the Israelis. Whereas Yasser Arafat reportedly authorized payments of $2,000 per "martyr," Saddam was said to have promptly paid the families of each Palestinian killed in the uprising

$10,000—a sum eventually increased to $50,000—with each Palestinian injured receiving $2,000. These payments were said to have been distributed mainly by members of the Arab Liberation Front, a faction of the Palestine Liberation Organization established by Iraq in 1969.

As the violence dragged on, Saddam continued to offer both rhetorical and substantive assistance to the Palestinians. At one point, Iraq sent a convoy of sixty-eight trucks containing food and medicine to the West Bank via Jordan. Another time, Saddam offered to "shell Israel daily for six months" to help the Palestinians.[36] Then, during the March 2001 Arab Summit in Amman, Saddam pledged to provide the PA with 1 billion euros—equivalent to $900 million—from the proceeds of the UN Oil-for-Food oil sales to fund the ongoing violence.[37] Later that summer, reports of Iraqi military assistance to the PA appeared in the Israeli press.

In September 2002, Israeli intelligence publicized documents captured from Arafat's headquarters in Ramallah detailing Iraqi involvement in the Palestinian violence.[38] When combined with interrogations of Palestinian terror suspects, these documents demonstrated a sustained pattern of training as well as operational and financial assistance from Baghdad.

All these initiatives—even if some were only empty pledges—boosted Saddam's popularity among Palestinians. Iraqi flags were frequently sighted at Palestinian demonstrations and martyrs' funerals, and families of the dead often sent thank-you notes to Saddam published in the local PA media. That the distant Arab "Saladin" in Baghdad, and not the much closer Arab king in Amman, was the object of so much Palestinian adulation heightened fears in Jordan that the Kingdom's Palestinian population—not just its large Iraqi expatriate population—might be a fertile ground for Iraqi political intrigue against the Hashemites.

CONCLUSION

Given the Jordanian–Iraqi rapprochement, the beleaguered remnants of the Iraqi opposition in Jordan unsurprisingly kept a low profile. While the Iraqi National Accord (INA) office in Jordan seemed to be busy with an active public relations campaign, a U.S. official in Amman confided that the opposition was in fact not "making a very big splash" and that it certainly was not broadcasting radio programs into Iraq.

While King Abdullah's tacit permission for the INA to stay in Amman essentially reflected continuity with his father's policy, over time the activities of the INA office atrophied. It seems the withering of the Iraqi opposition inside Jordan reflected official government policy. In this, Jordan appears to have been following the U.S. lead at the time. Whereas the George W. Bush administration adopted a policy of robust support for the Iraqi opposition in the wake of the September 11, 2001, attacks, it is important to recall that in the years prior to the al-Qaeda attacks, both the Bush administration and its predecessor kept the Iraqi opposition effectively at arm's length. Indeed, despite bipartisan support for the Iraq Liberation Act, which was enacted with President Clinton's signature, and despite bipartisan endorsement of the objective of "regime change" in Iraq, both presidents offered only tepid support to the Iraqi opposition, pre-September 2001.

This U.S. ambivalence toward the opposition was compounded by expressions of outright contempt made by King Abdullah during his April 2001 visit to Washington. In a speech before the National Press Club, he said: "It surprises me that such a weight has been put toward the opposition, and that there is an attitude that they're a solution. . . . I don't think they are."[39] Given then limp U.S. support for the Iraqi opposition and the unease the king must have felt in trying to balance between his U.S. security patron and his Iraqi economic lifeline, critiquing the Iraqi opposition was an easy policy choice. It did little, however, to mitigate the real threat Iraq continued to pose to Jordan.

Despite Abdullah's best efforts to improve Jordanian–Iraqi bilateral relations, signals persist that all is not well between the two states. For example, Iraq retains its haughty, disdainful view of Jordanians, on display during Prime Minister Abu Ragheb's visit to Baghdad in October 2000. According to observers, after Abu Ragheb was greeted on the tarmac for the benefit of television cameras, he was ushered away, the red carpet was removed, and the balance of the Jordanian delegation was herded off the plane and dispatched three to a room in a Baghdad hotel. News of the mistreatment of this high-ranking delegation made the rounds in the Amman rumor mill but received no press attention.

A more serious crisis emerged in early 2001, when the Arab press reported that Egypt, Syria, and Tunisia had signed (or were in the process of signing) FTAs with Iraq. Soon, there was much media speculation as to when Jordan would follow suit.[40] But the prospect of free trade with Iraq presented Amman with an obvious dilemma vis-à-vis Washington, so the decision was deferred; by March, the idea no longer dominated the headlines. Amman's hesitancy was not welcomed warmly in Baghdad, and the Iraqis showed their disfavor by sharply cutting imports of Jordanians goods. (Jordanian exports to Iraq declined by 18 percent during the first four months of 2001).[41] At the same time, Iraq and Syria registered a notable warming of their long frigid ties, exemplified by the frequency of official Iraqi visitors using Damascus as their travel hub to third countries, and by a rekindling of Syrian–Iraqi trade.

A third episode of Jordanian–Iraqi friction occurred in the context of the Arab League Summit in Amman held in March 2001, seven months into the Palestinian uprising. In the run-up to the meeting, Saddam launched a fierce rhetorical campaign against Jordan, going so far as to call on Jordanians to rise up and topple their regime.[42] No doubt, the budding rapprochement had reached its limit. To cap it off, Baghdad announced in May 2001 that it would suspend all oil transfers to Amman if the Kingdom endorsed the Bush administration's proposed revisions to the UN sanctions regime against Iraq, known as "smart sanctions."[43] Indeed, the king never publicly wavered from his advocacy of resuming arms inspections as a mechanism for "defusing tensions" and lifting sanctions. But in the end, Jordan was never penalized by the United States, and the Bush administration quickly withdrew its controversial and short-lived policy trial balloon.

NOTES

1. "Jalalatu yughadir ila Muscat al-yawm waminha ila al-Emirat," *Al-Dustur*, April 10, 1999.
2. *ABC News with Peter Jennings*, May 19, 1999.
3. "Jordan's New Monarch Speaks His Fill," Interview with King Abdullah from *Al-Hayat*, May 12, 1999, in *Mideast Mirror*, May 12, 1999.
4. "Jordan Reportedly Asks the Iraqi Opposition to Leave," *Al-Majd*, August 30, 1999, cited in Federal Broadcast Information Service–Near East and South Asia (FBIS-NES-1999-0830), August 31, 1999.
5. "Iraq Said Seeking Jordan Mediation with U.S.," *Al-Sharq al-Awsat*, October 5, 1999, cited in FBIS-NES-1999-1005, October 8, 1999.
6. "Jordan's King Not Carrying 'Specific' Iraqi Message to the U.S.," Agence France Presse, October 7, 1999, cited in FBIS-NES-1999-1008, October 13, 1999. This sentiment was echoed by the Jordanian ambassador in Washington, Marwan Muasher, who stated: "We want to emphasize that the King is here to discuss Jordanian themes, not to plead the Iraqi case."
7. "King Reiterates Call for End to Suffering of Iraqi People," *Jordan Times*, November 18, 1999.
8. "Jordan Restricts Iraqi Oppositionists' Activities," *Al-Sharq al-Awsat*, January 25, 2000, cited in FBIS-NES-2000-0125, January 27, 2000.
9. Bassam Badreen, "Al-Urdun yad'u liijwa al-tadamin al-sha'abi' maa al-Iraq," *Al-Quds al-Arabi*, April 10, 2000.
10. "DOD News Briefing," April 4, 2000, on Defense Link, www.defenselink.mil, February 13, 2003 [accessed February 14, 2003]. Secretary Cohen also took the opportunity of the press conference to highlight Jordan's strategic cooperation with Turkey and Israel—another unpopular subject in the Kingdom.

11. "Al-Qalab la tadakhul fi sh'uun al-Iraq wa la munwarat musharikat maa Amirika wa Isra'il," *Al-Ra'i*, April 5, 2000.

12. "Jilalatu istiqbal Indyk wa Abd al-Qiyum wa wafdan yahudiyan Amrikiyyan," *Al-Dustur*, May 14, 2000.

13. Bassam Badreen, "Al-Urdun tudaris talaban Iraqiyyan biinhai hathar al-tayaran," *Al-Quds al-Arabi*, May 20, 2000.

14. "Jordan Seeks Explanation from Iraq over Execution of Jordanian Citizen," BBC Worldwide Monitoring, June 9, 2000.

15. "Lower House Seeks Information on Jordanian Executed in Iraq," *Jordan Times*, June 15, 2000.

16. Marwan Asmar, "Jordan Week," *The Star*, June 29, 2000. Asmar cites reportage from *Al-Itijah al-Mu'akis*, a controversial program on the al-Jazeera satellite channel.

17. Salameh Ne'matt, "Al-Iraq yatlub min al-Urdun al-samah birihlat jawiyya ila Baghdad," *Al-Hayat*, July 16, 2000. Bassam Badreen, "Ramadan yuhafaf al-tawtur maa al-Urdun wa yutalib bimubadarat did al-hisar," *Al-Quds al-Arabi*, July 17, 2000.

18. Abdel Bari Atwan, "Suriya satuwaqaa salam khilal aam . . . wa hadithu saghira wara tawatur al-ilaqat maa al-Iraq," *Al-Quds al-Arabi*, July 19, 2000. Interestingly, King Abdullah also mentioned in the interview that his two visits to the United States were quite different. On his first visit as king, he said, the U.S. administration and Congress were "quite angry" with his calls for an end to sanctions on Iraq. During his visit in July 2000, however, he discovered that the United States was more sympathetic to "looking for a way and means to find a solution for this impasse."

19. "Al-Iraq: Mashrua tarmim matar al-Basra wa tarkiz ala istikhdam mena al-Aqaba," *Al-Hayat*, August 2, 2000.

20. "Istaqbal wazir al-tijara al-Iraqi ra'is al-wuzara," *Al-Dustur*, August 29, 2000.

21. Bassam Badreen, "Al-hukuma al-Urduniyya taltazim al-samt iza intiqadat Baghdad," *Al-Quds al-Arabi*, September 14, 2000.

22. "Baghdad tadu al-hukuma al-Urduniyya litajahil imla'at al-safir al-Amriki," *Al-Quds al-Arabi*, September 13, 2000.

23. In fact, Jordan had been submitting regular requests to resume Amman–Baghdad flights since at least 1997. See "UN Turns Down Jordan's Request for Amman-Baghdad Flights," *Jordan Times*, March 27, 1999, cited in FBIS-NES-97-086, March 27, 1999.

24. "Iraq Urges Countries to Resume Trade, Air Links under UN Charter," Agence France Presse, May 10, 2000.

25. "Azar ila Baghdad al-ithnain al-Urdun yustabadil al-dolar bil-Euro fil-ta'amul maa al-Iraq," *Al-Dustur*, October 26, 2000.

26. "Remarks of His Majesty King Abdullah II to the Cairo Arab Summit," Jordan Information Bureau, October 21, 2000, http://www.jordanembassyuk.org/JIS/summit_final_address.htm [accessed February 14, 2002].

27. "Saddam ya'arib fi risala lil-Malik an al-taqdir lijuhud jilalatu lirafa al-mu'anat an al-shaab al-Iraqi," *Al-Dustur*, November 2, 2000.

28. Rana Awwad, "Jordan's Trade with Iraq Markedly Improves over 1st Ten Months of 2000," *Jordan Times*, December 19, 2000, cited in FBIS-NES-2000-1219, December 21, 2000.

29. Muhammed al-Najar, "Al-ilaqat al-Urduniyya al-Iraqiyya: Hal tanaqul min 'Al-Malaf' al-iqtisadi ila 'al-tansiq' al-siyasi?" *Al-Sabeel*, October 15, 2000.

30. "Iraqi Groups Urge Jordan to End 'Harassment' of Exiles," *Al-Sharq al-Awsat*, December 7, 1999, cited in FBIS-NES-1999-1207.

31. Eid al-Fayez, interview by author, detailed notes, Amman, Jordan, October 2, 1999.

32. Saad Hattar, "Iraqis to Be Exempt from Penalties for Violation of Labor, Residence Laws," *Jordan Times*, November 8, 2000.

33. "Mu'anat al-musharakin min al-wusul ila jisr al-Malik Hussein," *Al-Dustur*, October 26, 2000.

34. In a December 24, 2000, speech, King Abdullah cited "more than 260 marches and 165 demonstrations" in Jordan since the start of the violence.

35. Ma'moun Ayash, "Al-Iraq A'aad 'Abu Raghrib' ila Amman mubtasiman," *Al-Sabeel*, November 15, 2000. On his return to Amman, Abu Ragheb carried a letter from Saddam to King Abdullah covering the same issue.

36. "Saddam to PA: I Would Shell Israel for Six Months," *Jerusalem Post*, January 17, 2001.

37. "Nus al-bayan al-khitami liqima Amman," al-Jazeera, March 28, 2001, in Arabic, www.aljazeera.net, April 10, 2003 [accessed February 14, 2003]. Also in English in "Text of Final Statement Issued by Arab Summit in Amman," *Al-Ra'i*, March 28, 2001, cited in FBIS-NES-2001-0329, March 29, 2001.

38. CBS News, *60 Minutes*, September 29, 2002.

39. National Press Club Luncheon Remarks by King Abdullah of Jordan, National Press Club, Washington, D.C., April 11, 2001.

40. Salameh Ne'matt and Ibrahim Hamidi, "Al-Urdun ala khita Misr wa Suriyya wal-Iraq yufakik al-hisar bil-tijara al-hur," *Al-Hayat*, January 10, 2001.

41. Rana Awad, "Figures Show Downward Trend in Local Exports to Iraq," *Jordan Times*, June 12, 2001.

42. "Taha Ramadan: al-Saudiyya tamawil al-gharat al-Amrikiyya did al-Iraq" *Al-Quds al-Arabi*, March 26, 2001. See chapter 3 for a more detailed discussion of this matter.

43. Raghida Dergham, "Al-Iraq yuhadid biqita al-neft an al-Urdun wa Turkiya," *Al-Hayat*, May 15, 2001.

Conclusion

Jordanian–Iraqi Relations and Implications for U.S. Policy

With the exception of the United States, Iraq qualifies as Jordan's most significant bilateral relationship. For Jordan, as previous chapters demonstrate, the relationship with Iraq is a double-edged sword. It is a relationship that also presents Washington with significant policy challenges. In particular, it highlights the question of how the United States should manage its relations with an ally (Jordan) that has extremely close relations with a leading adversary (Iraq).

Regardless of whether the Bush administration pursues regime change or continues a policy of sanctions and containment, the U.S. policy objective should be to pull Amman into the anti-Saddam orbit. This is necessary to undercut Jordan's long-standing economic dependence on Iraq. It is also required in order to undermine the destabilizing influence of Syria (which in recent years has been pursuing its own political, economic, diplomatic, and military rapprochement with Saddam) and of those West and East Bank Palestinians who are aligned with Ba'thi Iraq. As the Bush administration focuses more on regime change, these goals take on added urgency.

POLICY RECOMMENDATIONS

Although regime change had been articulated in the Republican Party presidential platform prior to November 2000, it did not become a central element of Bush administration policy until the fall of 2002. No doubt, the reprioritization of this goal has significant implications for all U.S. regional allies, but these implications are perhaps most profound for Jordan.

Although King Abdullah made great efforts in the first two years of his rule to reconcile with Iraq, few in the United States today question the king's

107

Western orientation. Unlike 1990–1991, when King Hussein was compelled to toe a "neutral" line during the Gulf War, it is almost inconceivable that King Abdullah would not (quietly) align himself with the West if the United States decided to actively pursue a campaign to remove Saddam Hussein. In any event, like his father, Abdullah would likely find himself in a precarious position should the United States return to Iraq. For Washington, then, the key will be to minimize potential dangers for Jordan while preserving the Kingdom's role as a moderating regional force.

Given the Kingdom's economic realities, it is unrealistic to expect Amman to forgo its trade/aid relationship with Iraq without proven, guaranteed substitutes. Given the unpopularity of U.S. policy, it would be similarly unrealistic to expect Abdullah—in the face of domestic opposition and regional ostracism—to side publicly with U.S. military action against Iraq. Nevertheless, there is much that Washington can do to lessen Amman's dependence on Baghdad, strengthen Jordan's domestic stability, and bolster the king's natural pro-Western instinct in such a way that the Kingdom provides the quiet support critical to any regime change strategy. Among other things, an effective U.S. policy toward Jordan—with or without the prospect of regime change in Baghdad—should include the following elements:

Diminish Jordan's Economic Dependence on Iraq

Although steeped in history, symbolism, and rhetoric, Jordan's political relationship with Iraq today is best understood in economic terms. For Jordan, close economic relations with Baghdad are a matter of survival. Decreasing this economic dependence is the key to limiting Saddam's political influence in the Kingdom. Moreover, in the event that the United States moves to oust Saddam, a major economic void would quickly emerge in Jordan. Without immediate, significant U.S. intervention (even if only temporary), the resultant economic hardship could threaten the Kingdom's stability.

The October 2000 U.S.–Jordanian Free Trade Agreement (FTA) was one high-profile attempt by the United States to foster a more economically self-sufficient Jordan. Given the types of products that Jordan specializes in (phosphates, fertilizers, pharmaceuticals, and textiles), the country may have difficulty taking advantage of this agreement. Eventually, though, the real FTA payoff for the Kingdom will likely come in the form of increased foreign investment in joint ventures geared toward the U.S. market. Such an increase in trade with the United States would provide a significant boost to the ailing Jordanian economy and help to diversify the Kingdom's export markets. Clear signs have already emerged that the U.S. market could be a boon to Jordanian exporters. From 1998 to 2000, Jordanian exports to the United States increased more than 400 percent, from $18 million to $73 million. In the first half of 2002 alone, Jordanian exports to the United States totaled about $141.5 million. This increase, while impressive, still lagged behind Jordan's exports to Iraq, which amounted to $182 million during the same period.[1]

Recognizing the political uproar that would ensue from a total severing of economic links between Jordan and Iraq—not to mention the practical impossibility of achieving this goal in the foreseeable future—the United States should focus on diversification of Jordanian trade. This shift would help to shrink the relative significance of Iraq's slice of the pie. Two key areas to pursue in this endeavor would be Israel and the Gulf.

Jordanians routinely complain that they have never benefited from a "peace dividend" with regard to the peace treaty with Israel, because Israel has imposed numerous nontariff barriers to prevent Jordanian access to both the Israeli market and, more acute for Jordanians, the $2 billion Palestinian market. In some areas, the Jordanians have a just argument. Nevertheless, steps have been taken to ease these problems, and should the Jordanian business community decide to turn its full attention westward, it would find opportunities today that did not exist five years ago. For example, as a result of U.S. efforts, the list of Jordanian products allowed into the West Bank was expanded and some transportation barriers were removed. This translated into increased Jordanian trade with Israel, which more than doubled from 1998 to 2001, reaching a total of over $100 million over the three-year period.[2]

Continue U.S. Support for Economic Reforms

Since his ascension to the throne, King Abdullah has attempted to tackle Jordan's economic problems—including nearly 25 percent unemployment and four years of negative growth—through a concerted campaign to privatize major government industries, streamline bureaucratic procedures, and fight governmental corruption. Most significant, the Kingdom has embarked on a program of legislative reform geared toward establishing an environment more conducive to foreign investment and to improved business relations with Europe and the United States.

Objectively speaking, the Kingdom has come a long way. Several large, state-owned corporations—including the Jordan Cement Factories Company, Aqaba Railway Company, and Jordan Telecommunications—have been privatized. Royal Jordanian, the state-owned airline, was put on the auction block in 2000, but the sale has been partly delayed due to the downturn in commercial civil aviation resulting from the terrorist attacks of September 11, 2001. In line with the slated reforms, Jordan has also steadily increased its foreign currency reserves and initiated significant tax reform, including conversion of the general sales tax into a value-added tax.[3] This apparent commitment to the reform agenda has created some quiet confidence in the Kingdom, contributing to a small but positive growth rate.

Nevertheless, Jordan remains in a difficult economic state, and it will likely take several years for the Kingdom to accrue the full benefits of the current reforms. Meanwhile, in the short term these reforms will be painful. A good example of this phenomenon is the pharmaceuticals industry. As a prerequisite to Jordan's World Trade Organization membership, the Kingdom had to institute a number of intellectual property (IP) laws, which effectively undermined the Kingdom's ability to compete in this sector. In 2001, six Jordanian pharmaceutical companies reported combined losses of $14 million, in large part because the government declined to register dozens of pharmaceutical products submitted for licensure by the manufacturers.[4] In fact, the IP reforms have been so damaging that the Jordanian Pharmaceutical Manufacturers Association considered filing a lawsuit against the government in 2001.

Although some decline in Jordanian industries may be inevitable, the United States can play a role in mitigating the losses. For example, Jordanian generic antibiotics are currently being sold in Britain. With support from the Bush administration and the Food and Drug Administration, more of these drugs could someday make their way to the United States.

Of course, this type of assistance would constitute only one of many steps that the United States could take to support the Kingdom's reform efforts. Another such step would be to continue the pattern of increasing U.S. economic assistance in the form of Economic Support Funds (ESF). In 2000, Jordan's ESF totaled about $200 million.[5] Although this figure dropped off in 2001, it was increased in 2002 to $235 million (including supplementals) and was slated to remain constant at $250 million through 2004. The United States should also increase its level of nonfinancial assistance to Jordan, such as the provision of more wheat or other excess commodities.

In addition, whenever possible, the United States should do what it can to help Jordan meet its often challenging commitment to the International Monetary Fund (IMF). In 2001–2002, Jordan was in its third and final year of an extended arrangement with the IMF worth $164 million, and IMF officials were commending the Kingdom's performance. Still, meeting the agreed targets was a real challenge. In 2001, for example, the Kingdom faced difficulties in remaining below its IMF-mandated gross national product deficit threshold of 6 percent. The increased price of oil under the 2001 Iraqi oil protocol had added $170 million in expenditures to the bottom line of the Kingdom's budget. In order to generate adequate revenues to cover this expense and remain within the IMF's prescriptions, Jordan was compelled to pass the cost onto the consumer and raise gasoline prices.

Decreasing the Jordanian government gasoline subsidy had been an item on the IMF reform agenda from the very start. The volatility of global oil prices had proven a severe detriment to revenue predictability and accurate budget projections. Moreover, Jordanian officials cited the higher price of imported oil as a contributing factor in the 3 percent decline in gross domestic product from 1999 to 2000.[6] Given the domestic environment in Jordan and the reverberations of the Palestinian uprising, however, Jordanian officials were loath to increase the price of this staple product. Their hesitance was only reinforced by the Islamic Action Front's condemnation of the policy.[7] In fact, many observers feared that a gasoline hike could induce something akin to the 1996 bread riots. With this prospect in mind, the increase was initially postponed.

In July 2001, however, gasoline prices for consumers were increased by 15 percent. Despite some grumbling and a reported upswing in gasoline tampering, the anticipated upheavals did not come. Still, the amount of trepidation surrounding this measure points to the ongoing stability concerns in the Kingdom. It also highlights how Jordan's continued economic dependence enables Baghdad to manipulate domestic crises. Even if Saddam is removed and a friendly pro-Western government installed, this dynamic of dependence will likely remain an obstacle to the political and economic well-being of the Kingdom.

At present, there is little doubt that Saddam could precipitate an economic crisis in Jordan were he so inclined, and Jordan might once again find itself in the awkward position of having to postpone reform measures in order to preserve stability. Such a scenario is not difficult to imagine, for although the IMF recently extended its economic reform program through 2004, Jordan still holds some 7 billion JD of foreign debt.

To help insulate the Kingdom from incidents such as the 2001 gasoline crisis, the U.S. government (a 24 percent shareholder in the IMF) should continue to take a sympathetic view of Jordan's predicament. Although the United States should treat Jordan as a mature state that is responsible for its own debt, Washington should also take into consideration the inherent difficulties of being a moderate state sandwiched between the Palestinian Authority (PA), Iraq, and Syria.

To be sure, the various pressures on Jordan have affected the pace of economic development in the Kingdom and the payoff of economic reform. In November 2000, for example, instability in the PA (and the overflow of unrest into Jordan) apparently caused the cancellation of a $100 million American manufacturing venture in the Kingdom.[8] Congressional approval of the U.S.–Jordanian FTA, which came in September 2001, will help mitigate this problem. High-level trade delegations led by senior Bush administration officials would constitute another positive sign. So long as King Abdullah proves that he is committed to the idea of reform, it is in the interest of the United States to lend this effort moral and material support.

Deepen the U.S.–Jordanian Military Relationship

Washington's military ties with Amman date back to the 1950s. This aspect of the bilateral relationship has varied over time—a fact perhaps best reflected by severe fluctuations in the levels of U.S. military assistance, or Foreign Military Funding (FMF), to the Kingdom (see table 5.1).[9] In 1976, for example, the United States provided $137.7 million in FMF to Jordan. In the years following the 1991 Gulf War, however, this assistance dropped to less than $10 million per year. After Jordan signed its 1994 peace treaty with Israel, FMF levels increased once again.

From 1996 to 1998, U.S. military assistance to Jordan was largely devoted to the lease and upgrade of F-16 Falcon fighter aircraft, a program close to the heart of the late King Hussein, but often criticized by observers as costly and inappropriate. More recently, though, the focus of FMF and military drawdown has shifted toward the modernization of the military, particularly the upgrade of border security equipment. For fiscal year (FY) 1999, the United States budgeted only $45 million in FMF for Jordan. In March 1999, then assistant secretary of state for Near Eastern affairs Martin Indyk made the case for increased military (and economic) aid to Jordan under the terms of the supplemental package created under the October 1998 Israeli–Palestinian agreement at Wye River. In his remarks before the Senate Appropriations Committee, Indyk stressed the need to "address the severely degraded conditions of basic military items" in the Kingdom.[10] "Jordan" he said, "can't defend its borders with Syria and Iraq without this equipment." Under the

Table 5.1. FMF Military Assistance (Including Supplementals) to Jordan ($ in Millions)

1991	20
1992	20
1993	9
1994	9
1995	7.3
1996	100
1997	30
1998	50
1999	95
2000	225
2001	75
2002	140

terms of the Wye supplemental, an additional $200 million was added to the FMF budget allocated to Jordan over a two-year period, with $50 million added to the FY 1999 budget (bringing the FMF total to $95 million) and $150 million added to the FY 2000 budget (for a total of $225 million).

In addition to providing equipment to Jordan—including Blackhawk helicopters (and upgrades to other helicopters), antitank missiles, communications technology, and border security gear—the U.S. military participates in several joint training exercises with the Jordanian military, most prominently the annual "Infinite Moonlight" and "Early Victor" exercises.[11] The bilateral training schedule is among the most robust in the U.S. Central Command's area of responsibility. Likewise, Jordan is among the most active participants in the International Military Education and Training program, under which foreign troops are trained and educated in the continental United States.

Indeed, from 1997 to 2000, U.S. military aid to Jordan increased to the point that FMF assistance to the Kingdom became comparable to the per capita annual U.S. military assistance provided to Egypt (i.e., about $20 per person per year). The Wye supplemental was a much-needed boost, but regrettably, 2000 was its final year.

Given Jordan's urgent military needs, the United States needs to do more.[12] Jordan has serious problems controlling its borders and faces significant threats—from smuggling to terrorism—from most of its neighbors. The border with Iraq has long been a problem, as has the northern border with Syria. For example, during the Sharm al-Shaykh terrorism summit in 1996, King Hussein presented Syrian president Hafez al-Assad with the files of dozens of apprehended Syrian intelligence operatives who had infiltrated Jordan allegedly in order to create mischief. The growing political, economic, and military rapprochement between Syria and Iraq—which could signal the reemergence of a rejectionist front on moderate Jordan's borders—heightens the peril for the Kingdom. The dramatic increase of infiltration attempts since September 11, 2001, from Syria and, to a lesser extent, Iraq highlights the continuing problem that these states pose. Deepening radicalism in the PA likewise exacerbates the dangers for Jordan.

To counter these very real threats, the United States should significantly increase its funding to bolster Jordan's ability to police its borders, in addition to continuing its already robust program of joint training and exercises. Of course, a higher-profile U.S. presence on Jordanian soil might generate some local backlash. Indeed, in July 2000, Jordanian Islamists condemned an Eastern Desert well-digging project sponsored by the U.S. Army Corps of Engineers as a precursor to the establishment of a U.S. military base.[13] Overall, though, the benefits that an upgraded military relationship and more secure borders could hold for the domestic stability of Jordan should not be underestimated.

Although the $75 million baseline FMF to Jordan for FY 2002 and FY 2003 is relatively low, there are some preliminary signs that this funding may be increased via supplementals and other mechanisms. In 2002, Jordan was slated to receive some $65 million over and above its $75 million baseline FMF—$20 million in Department of Defense, Defense Emergency Relief Funds, $25 million as part of the 2002 supplemental, and $20 million in war against terrorism coalition support funds. Given the active role that Jordan is currently playing (and will likely continue playing) in the campaign against terror, the Kingdom will probably be provided with additional funding in FY 2003 as well. Jordan's FMF for 2003 is already slated to increase to $198 million, and preliminary funding recommendations for 2004 point to another possible increase, to $206 million.

Reopen the Gulf

In lieu of the rather meager returns promised via trade with the United States and Israel, the most realistic alternative for Jordan is to turn to the Gulf. Prior to the 1990–1991 Gulf crisis, the Kingdom had reasonably positive relations with the Gulf states. Jordanian expatriate laborers worked throughout the Gulf, while Saudi Arabia provided the country with oil at preferential rates. These relations collapsed, however, with the Iraqi invasion of Kuwait and the subsequent Gulf War, when Jordan declined to participate in the international coalition against Iraq and was perceived as too sympathetic to Baghdad. The result was mass expulsion of Jordanian workers, severance of economic (and sometime diplomatic) ties, and closure of trade access to Gulf markets. The loss of workers' remittances alone amounted to about $1 billion per year.

Although the urgency of restoring Jordanian–Gulf ties was apparent throughout the 1990s, the United States rarely invested time and energy in this effort. Although numerous officials raised the matter of readmitting Jordanian expatriate workers and initiating oil sales to Jordan at discounted prices, such issues rarely reached the highest levels of U.S.–Saudi decision making, for example. Instead, when the United States sought Saudi assistance in the Arab–Israeli peace process, such support was usually defined in terms of aid to the Palestinians, not to the Jordanians. As a result of this prioritization, the Saudis routinely rejected U.S. entreaties to assist the Kingdom.

King Hussein's death and his son's accession opened a new window of opportunity to renew Jordanian–Gulf ties. Washington supported this effort, but the renewal was primarily King Abdullah's initiative. In March 1999, the Jordanian embassy in Kuwait, closed since 1990, was reopened. Meanwhile, the United Arab Emirates and Oman restored some assistance to the Jordanian military. For its part, Saudi Arabia sanctioned increased access for some Jordanian goods, even signaling a willingness to permit the entry of Jordanian workers, though not on any preferential basis. Moreover, following the March 2001 Arab Summit in Amman—during which King Abdullah attempted to broker a rapprochement between Iraq and Kuwait—Jordanian–Kuwaiti ties improved dramatically. A month later, following a visit by King Abdullah, Kuwait permitted the entry of numerous Jordanian workers. Oman and the United Arab Emirates soon followed suit.[14]

Although these have all been positive steps for Jordanian–Gulf relations, their economic value still pales in comparison to that of the discounted and free oil provided to Jordan by Iraq. As of the fall of 2002, the Gulf states continued to turn a deaf ear to Jordanian and U.S. entreaties regarding this issue. Often, Gulf leaders emphasize how expensive it would be to match Iraq's generosity. But another key element underlying the reluctance to supplant Iraq as Jordan's economic patron is the historical Saudi antipathy toward the Hashemites. As one U.S. diplomat pointed out, it is almost axiomatic that Riyadh likes to see Amman squirm.

Of all the reasons that Gulf states refuse to supply Jordan with oil at preferential rates, the most salient has probably been the widely held perception in the region that the United States lacked the will to pursue (let alone persevere and prevail in) its policy of regime change in Iraq. From the perspective of U.S. allies in the Gulf, the United States has permitted the erosion of UN sanctions, the expulsion of weapons inspectors, and the rearming of Saddam's military. Seeing the tide turn in Saddam's favor, these allies reacted accordingly, covering their bets by refusing to side openly with U.S. rhetoric on Iraq. In this process, no Gulf leaders were willing to risk Saddam's wrath by stepping in to serve as Jordan's economic champion; there was simply no percentage in it for them.

The Bush administration's reinvigorated Iraq policy—a concerted effort to implement regime change—stands a good chance of compelling a change of heart in Arab capitals. At least that was the dynamic that followed on the robust U.S. commitment of troops to evict Saddam from Kuwait in 1990. A similar signal of U.S. determination today may have the same effect on Arab leaders' overall Iraq posture and, more specifically, on their view of oil assistance to Jordan.

In the absence of a reinvigorated economic relationship between Jordan and its Gulf neighbors, the Kingdom will likely have to contend with Iraq for some time to come. Were it not for Saddam, Jordan could well survive on this dependence; after all, Jordan has been dependent on external sources of aid since its birth. But to the extent that Saddam poses an urgent threat to U.S. interests, so too does he pose a looming danger to moderate, pro-Western, pro-peace Jordan, popular perceptions inside the Kingdom notwithstanding. As the United States moves toward implementing a policy of regime change in Iraq, the economic and political difficulties for Jordan will be compounded.

Taking steps now to alleviate these dangers should be a central objective of U.S. Middle East policy.

U.S. support for Jordan could also facilitate political transition in Iraq. Indeed, by strengthening a Hashemite system that enables values of tolerance and moderation to take root in impoverished, weak, and largely resource-free Jordan (despite the Kingdom's persistent political and economic problems), the United States would implicitly be delivering a powerful message regarding what is possible next door, in a post-Saddam Iraq capable of fully exploiting its ample human and natural resources. Such a new Iraq—whether it developed into a democratic federal system under a republican regime or even a constitutional monarchy under a Hashemite restoration—would then become the friendly, vibrant, productive neighbor that Jordan and the entire Middle East have long desired.

NOTES

1. Sana Abdullah, "Iraq Beats U.S. as Jordan's Export Market," United Press International, August 27, 2002.

2. *IMF Direction of Trade Statistics Yearbook* (Washington, D.C.: International Monetary Fund, 2001–2002).

3. See Jordan's *Memorandum on Economic and Financial Policies 2001*, www. imf.org/external/np/loi/2001/jor/01/index.htm [accessed February 15, 2003].

4. Dina al-Wakeel, "Drug Manufacturers to Seek Legal Counsel in IPR Dispute before Gov't. Takes Action," *Jordan Times*, June 12, 2002.

5. "U.S. Assistance to Jordan," statistics compiled by the embassy of the Hashemite Kingdom of Jordan, www.jordanembassyus.org/new/aboutjordan/uj1.shtml, March 2003 [accessed February 15, 2003].

6. *Memorandum on Economic and Financial Policies 2001*.

7. See, for example, "Jabhat al-amal al-Islami tahathir min khatura rafa asa'ar al-mahruqat," *Al-Sabeel* (Jordan), July 3–7, 2001.

8. William Orme Jr., "Jordan Struggles to Keep Ties to Israel," *New York Times*, October 2, 2000.

9. Table 5.1 adapted from Alfred B. Prados, *Jordan: U.S. Relations and Bilateral Issues*, Congressional Research Service Issue Brief, updated March 20, 2001.

10. Martin Indyk, testimony before the Senate Appropriations Committee, Subcommittee on Foreign Operations, Washington, D.C., March 25, 1999.

11. The annual exercise slated for June 2001 was not completed due to concerns that Osama bin Laden might order an attack against U.S. troops in the Middle East.

12. In 2001, King Abdullah reportedly sold off longtime Hashemite holdings in Mecca for approximately $67 million in order to provide salary increases to his armed forces.

13. Suleiman al-Khalidi, "U.S. Army Ad Draws Fire from Islamists, Leftists," *Jordan Times*, July 2, 2000.

14. Oula al-Farawati, "Three Gulf States Finalizing Negotiations for Hiring Jordanian Teachers," *Jordan Times*, July 4, 2001. Interestingly, at the same time, the London Arab Press was reporting that Abdullah might also visit Iraq. See "Al-ahl al-Urduni yazur al-Kuwait wa ihtimal al-Iraq aydan al-shahar al-muqabil," *Al-Sharq al-Awsat*, April 25, 2001. Moreover, it bears noting that the new terms of employment for Jordanian expatriate laborers differ significantly from pre–Gulf War days. Teachers' contracts, for example, are now negotiated directly between the countries' ministries of education rather than as individual service contracts. This is widely seen as a disadvantage for the worker. Still, the prospect that thousands of Jordanian workers could return to the Gulf is a hopeful sign for the Kingdom.

Appendix A

Saddam Hussein's Letter to the Arab Summit, March 27, 2001

In the name of God, Most Gracious, Most Merciful

Dear brothers,

Peace upon whoever says: and peace and God's mercy upon you. . . .

"Our Lord, decide thou, between us and our people in truth, for thou art the best to decide." The Holy Kuran, VII, 89

The deepest point of the deep sea begins from the shore and then extends to reach there. This is why an introduction and some examples are necessary for delivering the idea. . . .

And because the basic aim of my address is to have some effect on you and to be affected by you through interaction with you, so that we achieve common action in the service of our Arab Nation which consists of our countries that represent it in different degrees according to their deeds, or to what they imagine and think. So please be patient and bear with me the introduction, examples and also stipulations because any one of us, kings and presidents, or of any other names and titles, cannot achieve what he wants, and all what we wish for our people and Nation, without bearing and being patient with each other in fairness so as our patience be a noble patience. . . .

We are, dear brothers, Arabs, are we not?! I do not think that anyone of us who are gathered here, or those who have not come here and have the same titles, would say the contrary. This means that our countries and the people in them belong to the same nation, and that we are believers in God. Nobody among us would go astray and say that this does not apply to him because he is not a believer, isn't that so?

So, our people's doctrine in life and politics, their psychological disposition, the way they are expected to act, the nature of their stands vis-à-vis events and their assessments of these events in all our countries, are all essentially so formed as to make their colour based on these two realities: Faith and Arabism. They are the wings without which our Nation cannot fly high in the sky, just as a bird without wings would be the prey of the lions of the universe. Who does and says the contrary?!

The man addressing you is a faithful Arab from Iraq. Iraq, dear brothers, is neighbouring two countries which are of the biggest countries or rather are the biggest, on the direct Arab periphery. They are two foreign countries. Whenever the Arab Nation wanted, or wants to show them the right way, it would turn to Iraq to do so. Whenever the Nation wanted to push away any evil coming from them, it would turn to Iraq just as Iraq turns to the Arab Nation whenever there is any harm coming to it from them. This was the right description of all the events that Iraq or the Arab Nation witnessed whether before or after Islam. Hence, Arabism and Faith became the basis of Iraq's existence and persistence, the basis for helping others to exist. Their stipulations have acquired analogies linked to this, so as any flexibility that does not achieve their goals and themselves, are rejected by Iraqi norms. Iraq would not deal with them and in many instances would revolt against them.

It is in this way that Iraq, which is your country, looks, dear brothers, to the corollary between the existence on one side and the Faith and Arabism on the other side. It is in this way that Iraq sees the inevitable corollary between Faith and Arabism or Arabism along with Faith. Allow me, hence, to give you some examples that confirm what I am saying:

You know, that the July 1958 revolution was a revolution of the people and the army, carried out by the people and the army after having made generous sacrifices. In its forefront was General Abdul Karim Kassim who led its military part. In addition to that he was of the highest military rank among the men of the revolution. Nevertheless, when he neglected Arabism and Faith, or did not make them the source of inspiration in patriotism and in the practice of the politics, the people revolted against him and punished him by shooting him in Al-Rashid street in October 1959, i.e., fifteen months after the advent of the revolution. Our people punished Abdul Karim Kassim, the leader of the revolution because he deviated from the concept of Arabism and Faith and then finished on him and on his regime on Feb. 8, 1963, i.e., four years after the advent of the 14th of July revolution which he led against the pro-Western regime. Before that, during aggression against Egypt in 1956, the Arab blood of the demonstrators against the regime was shed in Baghdad because that regime was the friend or follower of colonialism. Blood was shed, demonstrators took to the streets, lists of volunteers to support the people of Egypt were organized in the Arab countries, and the thrones and regimes were jolted by the ire of the Arab public. Before that the same stand was taken regarding the Algerian revolution against colonialism. And, on June 5, 1967, the same situation recurred in the Arab Nation's revolution against the aggression. Syria lost part of its territories and made sacrifices. Egypt lost part of its territories as well as Gaza and made sacrifices. Jordan lost the West Bank and Al-Quds. Iraq made sacrifices on both fronts, and the graves of Iraqi martyrs are still visited by Palestinians and Jordanians. There are also Iraqi martyrs in Syria. Never have the countries of the front confronted the Zionist entity in a war without Iraq being in the heart of it. The Palestinians have made so much sacrifices that they have acquired the right to be described, just as it has become a duty for us to describe their present stand as that of heroes of Jihad for confronting the American-Zionist weapons of destruction with stones. . . .

Hasn't all this taken place under the pressure of the two basic factors we mentioned and their correlation of Arabism and Faith? Aren't they the basic motivators and driving force behind all these sacrifices?

If the answer is like our answer, and that of all the Arab public: Yes! Then let's continue dealing with our Arab issues on the basis of this yardstick, without changing our obligations which stem from God's order and the prophet's teachings ordained by God on and for us, and which were chosen by men of good will as their path. Hence, we become the best successors of the best predecessors. Let's remember that Salah Al-Din Al-Aioubi wouldn't have liberated Palestine from the foreigners of the Crusades, hadn't he and his army had faith in the corollary between Arabism and Faith and their presence in their souls, conscience, and minds. These two factors are the motives that have pushed seven million Iraqis to volunteer for the liberation of Palestine. They form Al-Quds army that consists of twenty-one divisions to start with.

Do you realize, dear brothers, what does it mean to have seven million volunteers, or even if the number was less than that, from outside the army, to

contribute to the liberation of Palestine? Let me present to you some preliminary remarks to help you understand this fact:

They have volunteered with full awareness of what a war means, for they
have been fighting for about twenty years. Many men have been injured in
the battles of Al-Qadissya and Umalmarik (the mother of all battles). In addition to that, volunteering means not being able to fully provide for one's
family because the volunteers have to stop working which means, if they are
not public servants, not having any income to feed their children from the
sweat of their brows under these difficult conditions of the unjust blockade.
Nevertheless, they have volunteered for Palestine and its crown Al-Quds.

Do you give us reason, now that you know why we do not accept any bargaining on Palestine, all Palestine from the river to the sea, and from the sea
to the river, with its crown Al-Quds?!

By God we will bring them with an army whose end will be in Baghdad and
its forefront will be making the criminal Zionist invaders and occupiers'
blood run cold. If you want that and decide it, you will have an army of men
keen on wining martyrdom just as the Zionists are keen to live.

God will not disappoint the Arab Nation when it recalls the basis of its right
stand and action: Arand Faith. God is the greatest.

Dear brothers,

To conclude, we say that the yardstick to measure the stand of any Arab regarding the corollary between Faith and Arabism and the correlation of Faith
and Arabism which is his stand vis-à-vis two issues which we see as one: Iraq
and the blockade on one side, and the Palestinian people's struggle for the liberation of their territories. Any disregard of these two issues means disregarding the common basis on which rises the Arab Nation's stand that en-
deavors to have a prosperous and serene present and a guaranteed future the
disregarding of which would also be considered as disregarding the will of
our people in our countries.

Each and every one of you should be aware of the reality of the people in the
country in which he is the ruler.

Any disregard of the reality of the stand of the people from now on, in these
issues in any country on the part of the ruler who rules that country means

nothing but playing the role of the foreigner by proxy. He alone will bear the responsibility of his stand before God, the people, and history.

Finally, I would like to explain that in saying this I have no intention but to help those who hope or expect us to help each other, and encourage themselves to do whatever pleases God and bestows glory onto our Arab Nation. We aim also at mobilizing efforts in a serious way for the liberation of Palestine. The seriousness of our action will be best displayed by supporting the heroic Palestinian Intifada by all kinds of support: first and foremost by putting ourselves and resources on trial on the basis of the corollary between Faith and Arabism. They were the basis of our Nation when it was and its basis to be. We should avoid focusing our attention on trivial things that have made us lose many chances.

God is the Greatest. . . .

God is the Greatest. . . .

Let the imperialist and Zionist enemies of our Nation be debased. . . .

May God damn the Jews.

Saddam Hussein

Tholhija 24, 1421 H.

Source: "President Saddam Hussein's Address to the Arab Summit," translation by the Iraqi News Agency, March 27, 2001.

Appendix B

Palm Oil Case Study

In 2000, ghee, or processed palm oil, was the Kingdom's second largest export to Iraq. Because ghee is almost solely processed in Jordan for export to the Iraqi market, it provides an interesting case study of bilateral trade relations. Indeed, perhaps more than any other commodity, the sales of ghee to Iraq since 1991 reflect the dynamic of the Jordanian–Iraqi trade relationship.

In the aftermath of the 1991 Gulf War, UN export restrictions left many large industries in Jordan idle. A major exception to these limitations was the sector that included vegetable oils and soap, which were initially categorized as acceptable under the trade protocol system monitored by the UN. Not surprisingly, this designation provided Jordan with a monopoly on the Iraqi market and resulted in a boom for Jordanian producers.

At the time of the Gulf War, the Iraqi market was consuming about 270,000 tons of ghee per year, of which Jordanian producers supplied about 120,000 tons, or slightly less than one-half of the total.[1] Between 1991 and 1996 when the Oil-for-Food program was instituted, Jordanian production capacity skyrocketed and the number of vegetable oil factories in the Kingdom increased from two to nine, boosting the annual capacity from 120,000 to 300,000 tons per year. This increased capacity was destined solely for the Iraqi market.

In 1996, however, ghee—characterized as a foodstuff—was shifted out of the trade protocol and put under Oil for Food. From that point on, tenders became more competitive, and Jordan lost its monopoly. Saddam started to use Oil-for-Food contracts as a tool to gain political support, and ghee was a prime example.

The ghee that Jordan traditionally exported to Iraq was produced from palm oil, a resource commodity with one major global producer, Malaysia. In terms of the finished product, Malaysian production costs were far below those of Jordan. In addition, Jordan had to incur shipping costs from Malaysia (for raw

125

palm oil) of $30–$35 per ton to Aqaba, overland transport costs (for the raw oil) of $25 per ton to the processing plant in Amman, and return shipping costs (for the processed oil) of $25 per ton to Aqaba prior to being hauled to Baghdad.

All told, the transit expenses for the Kingdom's producers came to approximately $85 per ton. With a total market price of $660 per ton, this additional $85 priced Jordan out of the competition. Starting the mid-1990s, Malaysia also had the added luxury of shipping directly to the Iraqi port of Umm Qasr. Not surprisingly, Malaysia began to trample the competition. Over and above the price difference, Malaysia has also provided Iraq with $45 million of revolving credit for the purchase of ghee under a Palm Oil Credit Payment arrangement.[2]

Notably, though, Iraq did not award ghee contracts solely based on price. Politics were clearly also part of Saddam's calculus, for after 1996, according to an industry insider, Iraq began awarding contracts to companies in China, Egypt, and Syria—countries that faced expenditure outlays similar to those of Jordan. It is rumored that since 1996 Iraq has also signed a few contracts to purchase this commodity from Russia.

For the Kingdom's ghee industry, the years subsequent to 1996 were disastrous. One company, which in 1995 sold about 12,000 tons per year for about $11 million, in 1997 sold only about 4,000 tons for $2.5 million. In the late 1990s, fearing a total collapse of the ghee sector, Jordanian industry leaders asked Amman Chamber of Industry head Khaldoun Abu Hassan to intervene with Baghdad on their behalf. Abu Hassan met with Iraqi minister of trade Muhammad Mahdi Saleh and secured a "subsidy" for Jordanian vegetable oil producers of $50 per ton to make the Kingdom's offers more competitive. In spite of this arrangement, the Jordanian palm oil processing industry continued to fail.

Although the Jordanian market share has declined precipitously since 1996, Iraq nevertheless continues to purchase the higher-priced Jordanian-produced commodity. As the Islamist weekly *al-Sabeel* noted in February 2000, Iraq continued to award palm oil contracts to Jordan "in spite of the fact that Malaysia has much lower prices."[3] Indeed, in February 2000, the Iraqi minister of trade indicated that Iraq had increased its imports of vegetable oil from the Kingdom by 50 percent under the previous phase of Oil-for-Food.[4]

Of course, from a strictly economic perspective, one might ask why Iraq would continue to purchase ghee from the Kingdom at all. Clearly, Baghdad's policy of subsidizing the existence of this relatively inefficient Jordanian industry does not make economic sense. But Jordanians are keenly aware that economics are not the bottom line for Iraq. The key, it seems, is politics, not economics. Ghee manufacturers and other industrialists comprise an important base of political support for Iraq inside Jordan and are an integral part of a network that Saddam has cultivated for nearly two decades. The slightly higher cost to Baghdad is inconsequential when compared to the goodwill that trade with this sector generates for Iraq. The community of businessmen and industrialists in the Kingdom is quite well connected and influential and plays a key role in Jordan's policymaking process. Likewise, Jordanian businessmen often serve in top government positions. Keeping the ghee industry subsidized is a small price to pay for all the benefits that Iraq accrues in return.

While Iraqi purchases determine the survivability of the ghee industry in Jordan, for China, Russia, Egypt, and Syria these contracts serve as a reward for supporting Iraq's efforts to secure an end to UN sanctions. As one Western diplomat in Amman described it, the increased Iraqi purchases of Malaysian-produced ghee since 1996 have been a "gift" to thank the country for its support for Iraq at the UN. In December 2000, to cement burgeoning relations and "further develop" strategic ties, Iraqi minister of trade Saleh visited Malaysia.[5] Iraq, which had already purchased some $500 million in Malaysian products under the UN Oil-for-Food program, was said to be interested in purchasing, in addition to other commodities, the Malaysian national car, the Proton.

NOTES

1. Interview by author with a Jordanian owner of a vegetable oil processing company, detailed notes, Amman, Jordan, October 5, 1999.

2. *Business Times*, (Malaysia), January 13, 2000.

3. Muhammed al-Najar, "Man hu al-mustfid min takhrib ilaqat al-Urdun wal-Iraq?" *Al-Sabeel*, February 15–21, 2000.

4. "Minister Views Trade with Jordan, Comments on Sanctions," *Al-Ra'i*, February 1, 2000, cited in BBC Summary of World Broadcasts, February 12, 2000.

5. "Iraqi Trade Minister in Malaysia, Vietnam," Radio Free Europe/Radio Liberty 3, no. 43 (December 22, 2000).

Appendix C

Text of Marwan Muasher's FTA Letter (to Members of Congress and the Bush Administration)

Embassy of the Hashemite Kingdom of Jordan
Washington, D.C.

Marwan Muasher
Ambassador

February 5, 2001

Dear Friend,

Last week, statements in Jordan on the issue of a free trade agreement between Jordan and Iraq were interpreted by some in the United States as a potential violation of UN sanctions against Iraq. I would like to set the record straight.

1. Jordan fully abides by all UN resolutions on Iraq, and will continue to do so. Jordan does not intend to violate any of these resolutions. In this regard, recent Jordanian flights to Iraq all had prior approval from the United Nations Sanctions Committee.

2. A free trade agreement with Iraq does not result in open trade while the sanctions regime is in place. It simply means a reduction of tariff rates on commodities approved by the UN Sanctions Committee. Any expansion of such commodities will necessarily have to wait until such a sanctions regime is lifted.

3. While Jordan continues to seek ways to improve its economic situation at a time of rising oil prices and a difficult political situation to its west,

any discussions on the issue of a free trade agreement with Iraq will not
be conclusive at this stage.

I hope you find this useful. I want to take this opportunity to thank you for
your continued support of Jordan during a particularly difficult time.

Sincerely,
Marwan Muasher
Ambassador

Index

Page numbers appearing in italics refer to the tables on those pages.

About the Author

David Schenker is Levant country director in the Office of the Secretary of Defense (International Security Affairs). In this capacity, he serves as primary advisor to the undersecretary of defense for policy on Syrian, Jordanian, Lebanese, Israeli, and Palestinian affairs. Prior to his appointment at the Department of Defense, Mr. Schenker was a research fellow at The Washington Institute for Near East Policy, where he specialized in Arab and Islamic politics. Before joining the Institute, he was senior researcher at the Investigative Project, where he wrote about terrorism and U.S. policy.

Mr. Schenker has written extensively about the Middle East. In 2000, he authored *Palestinian Democracy and Governance: An Appraisal of the Legislative Council* (The Washington Institute), and his scholarly articles and editorials have appeared in the *Los Angeles Times*, *New York Post*, *Jerusalem Post*, and *Middle East Quarterly*, among other media.

Mr. Schenker holds a master's degree in Middle Eastern studies from the University of Michigan (1992) and a bachelor's degree in political science and Middle Eastern studies from the University of Vermont (1990). In 1992–1993, he was a Center for Arabic Study Abroad (CASA) fellow in Cairo, Egypt. He speaks, reads, and writes Arabic.